THRIVING
WARRIOR

A Journey through Hospice with Cancer

KAREN LEWANDOWSKI

The Author has tried to recreate events, locales and conversations from her memories of them. In order to maintain anonymity in some instances she has changed the names of individuals and places, she may have changed some identifying characteristics and details such as physical properties, occupations and places of residence.

THRIVING WARRIOR

Copyright © 2015 by Karen Lewandowski

All rights reserved.

Edited by Kim Egan

Cover design by Susan Humphrey

Published by Thriver Publishing

ISBM-13: 978-1511585705

ISBN-10: 1511585706

DEDICATION

Dedicated to my love, Jay Kline. Without his support and love this book would have never have developed. Jay saw me through the worst of times and supported me through the writing of this story.

To my daughters; Kristina Lewandowski; Debbie Powell; Heidi Powell; Stefanie Powell; Victoria Wanaka, and my niece Tina Lewandowski for the strength of family and their desire for me to strive to live.

To Kim Egan, my editor and friend, Thank you for the suggestions on layout, wording, and the encouragement to just sit down and write. You allowed me the space to let the words flow while pushing me back when I was distracted from this story. You inspired me to keep my fingers on the keyboard.

To Gen Griffin, she wasn't afraid to hurt my feelings and challenge me to do more, one more time. We are better for knowing each other.

To Susan Humphrey, willing to take a last minute idea and run with it. Thank you for your faith.

Introduction

I am a cancer vixen! I am thriving with Stage 2 Invasive Ductal Carcinoma with Metastatic Disease also known as Stage 4 Breast Cancer. I am loved by Jay and my five daughters, Kristina, Debbie, Heidi, Stefanie and Victoria. I am blessed to be a grandmother to 12 wonderful grandchildren. I am also an advocate for responsible animal ownership, the rights of those individuals with disabilities and for metastatic disease funding and research.

I was initially diagnosed with breast cancer in the spring of 2006. My cancer returned in September 2010. The cancer cells had moved into my bones and the pleural lining of my right lung. My prognosis was dire and I was admitted to Life Path Hospice.

I posted a warning for cancer on my Facebook profile where I said: "I will stand back up! You'll know the moment when I have just had enough! Sometimes I'm afraid, and don't feel that tough, But. . . I will stand back up! Your time in this body is over! I am a cancer assassin and I will destroy you with all the tools and resources available to me!"

An amazing group of individuals began to flood in with prayers and support via social media and email lists.

Cancer fighting takes more than doctors, medications, chemotherapy, radiation, etc. It also takes laughter and staying at the party until the last cocktail is served! There were some mornings after I was released from the hospital that I would wake up and feel like I had the weight of the world pressing on my chest and emotions. On those mornings I had to recognize the pain for what it was and get out of bed to live my life! I resolved to not let my emotions become an enabler for failure.

I traveled through a 14-month journey with cancer as a constant internal companion. The cancer was not as strong as the support group I have. Through the treatments and while on hospice care, I continued to attend college, positively encourage others to reach for their dreams, advocate for animals and I continued living. Cancer was a bump in the road, a pretty big bump. This new condition will never conquer my spirit. I have resolved to learn something from it and not to accept the finality of life.

Millimeter-by-millimeter your life can change in a second. Surprises sneak in and change the direction of your thoughts. What you thought you knew becomes changed and irrelevant to the future. Live each second of your life a millimeter at a time and appreciate the beauty that disappears forever with the setting of the sun. Think of others first, and then lead with love. That is what makes a hero, a champion, a role model and mentor.

I am no longer a Life Path Hospice client. My cancer is medically controlled for the fourth time and I am currently receiving treatments which allow me to live my life. I graduated at the local community college with honors.

Breast cancer is a chronic medical condition, not an automatic death sentence.

Chapter 1

The Big C

The sun is shining as I walk down the driveway, out to the mailbox. The scent of freshly cut grass filled my senses. Our black mailbox is unremarkable. I reach into the back of it and remove a stack of mail. Based on the amount of circulars, it is Wednesday. I take a moment on the way back inside to walk barefoot through the grass. The blades tickle the bottom of my toes. Coolness wraps around the sides of my feet.

Mail from a doctor's office. This envelope is no great surprise. I recently had my first mammogram and this letter must be the results. With utter disregard to the contents I rip the flap of the envelope open. I have received a referral for a follow up mammogram and an ultrasound. Test results listed possible movement or other irregularity. A fleeting thought: I should have kept that appointment with my doctor last week. Regardless, all is well. I will not worry about next week and will try harder to be still during the next big squeeze.

On the day of my appointment, I'm relieved that I remembered how to get to the lab. The last time I was here I ended up being late. The medical area consists of five streets. Finding the right street, turning at the right location requires knowledge, timing and a slight degree of luck. Miss your turn and you can plan another trip around the block and the frustrations of the hospital traffic that the block surrounds.

I have to update my personal information when I sign in. No changes in the last few weeks. Life is finally normal and quiet. Registration will be my next stop, but first there is the usual sit down and hurry up and wait. It's a game. We've all been there and done that. Most of us have a medal for it. I will call Jay, my special guy, to let him know I have safely arrived. We can have a cup of coffee afterwards from the bagel shop down the road when the tests are completed. I can almost taste the rich brew of the French vanilla coffee that I like. Anticipation, it is always half the enjoyment of a great cup of coffee.

Registration. Okay, let's get this part over with. My name? Yes, I'm Karen Lewandowski. My health insurance is still the same. No changes in address. I'm here for what! What do you mean I have a mass! Darkness hovers at the edge of my vision. I can only see the registrar. All sounds become a dull hum behind me. I struggle to focus on what I am hearing.

"I want to see the results from the mammogram, please." I wait for her to go pull the report.

Fear, a dark encompassing gut-wrenching fear envelops me. I know without further testing that my mass is cancerous. I don't need to be told. Jay, I have to call him, he needs to be here now. Urgent, I need him here. He answers the phone right away and asks what is wrong. I'm scared I tell him that I need him here right now and he is talking to me as he walks out the office door. Hanging up I return my attention to the registrar, she has the report. It reads that I have a suspicious mass in the 12:00 position of my right breast.

It's been more than two minutes since Jay and I talked. Why can't he drive faster? Why are my cheeks wet? I'm not crying?

Jay my warmest safe haven, he's here. It felt like forever for him to arrive. His strong arms wrap around me. He holds me close. My cheek fits perfectly against the hollow above his collarbone. No matter what happens, I'm safe now. Together we can conquer any problems that come our way.

Another mammogram while Jay is waiting in the hallway. I can do this. This time the technician has to apply more pressure to compress my breast further. I'm pushed and pulled to get the plates right up against the ribs. 12:00 means dead center as far back as it can get and still be in breast tissue. I try hard to not complain, but I do want to know why they have to crank the plates together so fast. The technician stops and begins to manually crank the plates into position.

I'm escorted out into the hallway where Jay was waiting. The walls are barren and sterile. I reach for Jay's hand and grasp it like a lifeline.

The ultrasound is next. Jay continues to wait out in the hallway. This room is even more sterile than the halls, it is so quiet. I cannot get the ultrasound technician to engage in conversation. The pressure she applies causes discomfort but not as much pain as the mammogram plates inflicted. I have too much time to think. What's next? Cancer? The tests are done, but I have to wait for the results. They can take two weeks to come back. I know I have a suspicious mass. My gut says its cancer. I cry.

Okay, so cancer, I might have cancer. What's the worst that could happen? I could have cancer. Okay, well, if I have cancer what's the worst that can happen? I could die. And if I die, what's the worst that could happen? There is no "worse" than dying. That's it. That's final.

Okay then. It's time to start preparing for the worst and living for the best. We are escorted back to the changing area. I step into the room alone and slowly put my clothes back one. I stare at my breasts. What will it be like to have them both removed? I won't keep either one if there is cancer in one, I had made that decision 20 years ago. Breasts are not more important than my life.

Jay and I walk out to our cars. I no longer want a cup of coffee. I just want to call my mother and go home. Jay and I talk and decide that we are not going to borrow trouble. We need to wait for the results, after all this could be a non-cancerous tumor.

I hug Jay and send him back to work. I don't want to miss out on any of his hugs, not a single one. Whether I have a lifetime or part of a lifetime, his hugs make me smile. It's time to call my mother and get a grip.

Mom answers the phone at work. I go from being a grown-up who calls her mother "Mom" to her little girl calling for her mommy. I guess you never outgrow being your parents' child.

"Mommy I have cancer, they found a lump in my breast," I say.

"I'll be okay right? Help me make a plan, please Mommy?" I go on to explain that we are waiting for more results but I know in my gut that the mass is cancer. I need her to help me get centered.

Ingrown toenails.

Can you believe my mom has them also? Tumor, suspicious mass, cancer. She wants me to think of that the same way as I do of my ingrown toenails. Ingrown toenails are a nuisance but it is not like they are a death sentence. I dig them out, they bleed a bit, I put some Neosporin on, and I keep on going.

Okay so I have breast cancer. It's just like I have an ingrown toenail, just like other people get warts. I am going to have the doctors cut it out, treat it, and I'm going to keep on living. My mother reminds me that I have the power to control how things affect my life. She tells me not to let cancer or the threat of cancer have any power to ruin my life or to change my life.

"Thank you mommy, I love you."

I'm finally done crying. I have a plan. As we prepare to hang up, I remind her, "Mom you can't cry either, all right?"

Yeah, she really listened to that last part. Many days later, one of Mom's friends told me she didn't just cry at the news: she wept hysterically. According to her friend, the tears poured out of her eyes like a flood of water through a dry riverbed. My mom didn't understand why, of all of her daughters, I was the one who was going to have cancer. I didn't smoke. I didn't do drugs. I didn't drink in excess. Sometimes she was frustrated because I insisted we eat healthier foods "Why?" she asked. What went wrong? Even though she works in a doctors' office, they were unable to answer her questions. Although she was not alone, she felt totally forsaken. The medical community had failed her.

Now there can be no more tears. Driving past work, I pray. Not to bargain with God, just to make in a statement of facts. God, I have cancer. Fine! But it's your problem, and I am giving it to you hook line and sinker. I will do what the doctor says; you take care of everything else. From now on I have cancer like I have an ingrown toenail or other people have warts. I am going to have cut it out be done with it. I'm not sick. Cancer doesn't make you sick. I only have cancer and only on the days I have to be treated. Give me what I need to live through this. This problem . . . it is yours. I'm done with it! Got it? I'll talk with you again soon, thank you.

I've shifted that burden. It's done. I decide to call Jay and let him know that I'm on my way home. I'm fine. I love him.

After I arrived home, I called and scheduled more appointments with the doctors. I have to go get the results and find out what the next steps are. Little do I realize that these appointments are going to be among the first of many appointments for this year.

I return to my primary care physician. It's exactly as I thought. I have a suspicious mass of my right breast. It's time for referrals. Many referrals.

I begin to research my own condition. I need to know what questions I should ask the doctor who will be told to remove both of my breasts if I have cancer. The online research I did for that question alone resulted in a four page questionnaire. The obvious questions spring to mind, from successes to risks of complications to a double mastectomy versus a lumpectomy, but there are so many questions to ask that they not written down. I won't remember them. I hope I can trust this doctor and he can answer my questions.

I go in for more tests. So many, they blur together. Needle core biopsy. CT scan. MRI. All body scan. Blood work, endless blood work. I feel like a never-ending food supply for a vampire. Amid all these tests, Jay and I have made a firm decision. We are going to delay the surgery until the summer. It's not like I have to hurry up and remove my breast, the cancer is already there. Our girl graduates this year and we plan on being there to watch her graduate high school. Our breast surgeon agrees with our decisions.

Prior to leaving, I take all the test results and images to get a trusted family practice doctor to explain it in layman's terms. Without having the results of the biopsy completed I explain about how much the procedure hurt. With the information available at that moment in time

11

I am assured that there is less than a 15% chance I will have active cancer mass. Tumors that are cancerous do not result in pain in 85% of all biopsies. I find some small comfort in this statistic.

We went to California and Arizona. We visited with Jay's son and we watched our girl graduate high school. The weather in San Diego was delightful. I even took the time to get my haircut. Now that we are home, we will tackle first things first. Jay has to have his eye surgery. His retina detached while we were out West, and he is my top priority.

Chapter 2

I Am A Survivor

The surgery to remove my breast is scheduled for June. We begin interviewing the hematology and radiation oncologists. Hematology and chemotherapy. They say it's one in the same. My insurance chooses my oncologist for the chemotherapy. Off we go for an interview.

This doctor is almost in downtown Tampa a multistory building without enough parking. Jay leaves me at the entrance as he drives across the street to park our vehicle in the overflow parking. I wait. Waiting is something that I am becoming accustomed to now.

The oncologist is of Spanish heritage and practices the traditional male culture behaviors. He discusses my case with Jay as if I am not in the room at all. The singular interaction he had with me was that of a father to a small child. Some doctors just don't get that I am the person with cancer. I want them to talk to me. I am perfectly capable of asking questions, answering your questions and being involved in any decisions.

I use sign language to tell Jay that we are not going to use this doctor. He nods in agreement. We leave and discuss how to find another doctor to handle the chemotherapy treatments that I will need.

As we drive home I call my breast surgeon and ask him to recommend doctor for me. We get a referral to go see a different doctor, a woman. Insurance takes two weeks to get approval and schedule an appointment. We finally get to meet with her and spend almost ninety minutes of talking about my treatment. I decide I would like her. Again using sign language Jay and I confirmed that this woman will be a doctor that we will use for my chemotherapy treatments. Smiling she looks up at us and comments on our sign language conversation. I explain our last encounter and that we would like to have her on our medical team. My team is now three fourths complete.

The final step for the medical team is selecting a radiation doctor. It seems as if these interviews never stop! This doctor is down in Sun City Center. I walk in with six pages of questions. The doctor takes my six pages and I initially panic. She doesn't discard them. Instead, she starts with the first question and answers every single question on the list. I feel as if I'm batting 1000. We discuss the different types of radiation. She explains why some would work and some are not ideal. I walk away with the understanding that, overall, the biggest side effect of radiation treatment will be severe sunburn.

My surgery goes as planned and my breast is removed. When something wants to kill you get rid of it. The scar line, it's actually very beautiful. Nice and tight, even sutures, no angry row lines.

I start chemotherapy at St. Joseph's Women's Hospital in downtown Tampa as soon as I finish recovering from my surgery. They have individual rooms with beds. There is an open living area with a television, recliners, and paintings on the wall. I opt for the privacy of a single room with a bed and a private television. Today is my first treatment. The nurses are fantastic. They explain what the medication will do: nausea, hair loss, feeling tired. Heck, I can handle that. That's why I got my haircut. I'm counting the days until Jay and I can shave my head.

The nausea finally comes after I am home. Wave after wave of nausea. I can handle this. After all, I've been pregnant. It's nearing midnight I'm dehydrated, I'm so weak I can't even rollover to try to vomit while my body heaves. Jay has called the doctor and picked up some prescriptions to stop the nausea. Soon he'll have me feeling better. The remainder of the night passes without the nausea stopping. I wind up back in the hospital to be treated for dehydration.

My second treatment is again an experience. My port is not

accessed properly. I complain of pain and ask them to check it and I'm assured that it is in correctly and it is causing discomfort because this is only the second time it was accessed. The nurse was surprised to see a bulging in my chest where the fluid is building up in the subcutaneous tissue on my chest.

My two remaining chemotherapy treatments are not this eventful. With the proper premeds for nausea and post medications we were able to prevent the nausea from happening again and proper needle placement resolved the other issue. Chemotherapy, it became part of what I did, it did not control how I did it.

Radiation treatments last six weeks for a total of 30 treatments. I'll be done by the first of the year. Completion of the radiation will be the best New Year's gift I could get. I get slightly claustrophobic receiving my treatment. The actual treatment takes less than three minutes. I start off feeling like there's nothing to this. I would rather do radiation than chemotherapy any day of the week. Halfway through my radiation treatment, my skin where my right breast was begins to blister. Minor sunburn I expected that. Raw open oozing sores didn't expect that. I couldn't wear clothing on my chest. I couldn't do another treatment. I received several days break from the treatment. I now understand that my treatment will extend past January 1. But at this point it's worth the extra days.

As of January 2007, all of my treatments are done. I have a clean bill of health. I'm not a patient. I am a survivor. I've always been a survivor.

Chapter 3

Cancer Free and Living My Life

I have been cancer free since 2007. Cancer had reared its ugly head one more time in my life and brought MRSA along as a close companion. I become a caregiver to my mother when she was living with end stage pancreatic cancer in 2009. My mom went from being my support to needing my support. Her Whipple surgery was only partially completed because the biopsies on the tissue samples showed scar tissue and not cancer cells. This is one of the tricks of cancer it isn't everywhere in an organ, every time. By the end of May my mother had been recommended to Lifepath Hospice in Hillsborough County. Medicine and science had failed my mother yet again. She developed MRSA from the surgery to remove the cancer from her pancreas. The social worker from the hospice program was very concerned with making sure that our family had the resources we needed to give my mother the best life she could have. Her death was to be on her terms, not at the whim of some doctor in the hospital. Little did I know that I would meet this social worker again. July 8, 2009 my mother peacefully died. Her body had been wracked with pain in spite of the medications because of the systemic MRSA infection. We felt relieved that she was finally out of pain even though our grief was indescribable.

Our daughter and her son had moved to Florida to live with my mother before we found out that she had reached a non-treatable condition with the cancer. Jay and I now had a full house as my mom transferred custody and responsibility of her youngest daughter to Jay and me. Our home was instantly full with a daughter, grandson and niece plus two dogs. Believing that education is best taught by example I decided to complete my four year degree in business management. I applied to a local 4 year college and learned that although I did have an associate of science, my California courses would not transfer to provide me the credits needed for a 4 year degree. I had to begin again and earn my associate of arts degree so that I could then go on to eventually earn a master's degree. My first classes began at the local community college in the spring of 2010. Tina and I were both students together and would on occasion even do homework together.

I began my newest degree with a focus on the core classes, English, Math and Psychology courses. I was unable to grasp the concepts in the algebra class and was not successful in completing the course. It was a course that I would take over in the fall as summer classes were too short to provide the degree of instruction I would require. During the summer I was able to enroll in a full class load of 4 courses, public speaking, ethics, English composition, and general psychology. Even with this challenge I found time to visit with my friends and have fun.

Summer fun in Florida means Kayaks. This is one word that I never want to attempt to repeat in the same sentence as fun. It was a bright and cool summer morning when Ruth and I went kayaking. I did not know that boating in this type of boat would require deep squats and limited back support. When we arrived at our friends house on the river I bent down to pick up a dropped key and could barely stand back up from the immediate pain. I believed that I had pulled the muscles in my lower back and hoped that the warmth of the day would help relax them while we were out on the river. The pain continued when I got into the kayak and for the duration of the boat ride. I do not like back pain and I do not like kayaks that cause back pain to increase. I won't be doing this activity again in the future. For the next four nights I take a 2 mg dosage of Flexeral and move about like a zombie during the daytime. This affects my ability to think in addition to do simple household tasks. The pain is no longer just in my lower back but has extended to my entire spine and pelvis. I am not sure what would cause such an ache pain, it must have been the hard plastic seat of the kayak.

Eventually the pain decreased and I was able to continue with my normal activities. Our daughter Kristina had decided that after a year in Florida she wanted to return to California and be closer to the rest of her son's family and her friends. We began to make the arrangements for her to fly home and ship her personal belongings back to her when I found a new lump on the mastectomy scar line of my right chest wall. I began to prepare for the worst case scenario. What is the worst that could happen? Well that's easy – it could be cancer again. If it is cancer what is the worst that could happen? Again an easy answer, the worst that could happen is that I could die from it. But as we all know, the worst doesn't usually happen without a lot of warning. Death may come like a thief in the night, but it will not arrive on this night or any night in the near future.

I woke up trying to find a positive affirmation to live by for the day. Some days, because of the back pain, finding that positive affirmation to live by is harder than others. "Frogs have it easy. They eat what bugs them", I thought. I can't eat my worry. I needed to decide how to deal with sharing the information that I might be facing cancer again, before it is even diagnosed as a cancer. There is no right way to do a wrong thing. So how do I tell people I love that there may be more cancer? I had to decide if I was going to let them worry or wait until we knew if there was anything to worry about or not. Finally I decided that I would share my concerns with Jay and not seek any diagnostic treatments until after our daughter had arrived back in California. She needed to go "home" and I didn't want her to feel as if she had no options and was required to stay to take care of me.

There is no right answer to the question of waiting or sharing the information. All I could do was continue to take my summer classes and keep on keeping on. As the time gathered closer for Kristina to fly back to California I began to experience more pain in my spine and found it difficult to sit or walk. The discomfort was a constant nagging companion and required some serious accommodations whenever I went to sit down.

It was finally time to drive Kristina and our grandson to Miami so they could fly to California. They were so excited. Even Tina was excited about the weekend in Miami. Kristina shared on her Facebook page: "I can't believe it's almost time to go! 4 days left of work and I am done! I'm kind of really excited about this next step in life! It's amazing how the wrong people can show you how great the right people are! I am so blessed to have nothing but wonderful people in my life".

Now, I know I have made the right choice; any other choice would be a burden she does not deserve. During the trip to Miami I take the time to share with Jay about the lump on my chest. We agree that I will schedule my medical appointment with my breast surgeon as soon as he has an opening next month. I have lots to do with the fall semester starting and getting prepared for the algebra class I would be taking. This would be just one more activity to schedule.

I call and schedule the appointment to my breast surgeon shortly after my oldest daughter and her son moved back to California. The office wanted to get me in immediately, but I chose to make an appointment for a Friday when Jay would be home and could attend with me. Delaying the appointment from a Wednesday to a Friday will not change any significant issues that have already developed. It will allow me to be fully focused and prepared for the appointment.

In life there is No Secret Pill. There is No Magic Wand. When you want to make that change you can just say so and then sit back, or you can emotionally invest into yourself and make it so. Make your choice - Then live it! This semester I am taking a single class. Introductory Algebra is the name an A is the game! The professor is so calm and explains everything in a way that I understand. I'm maintaining an A so far in class. I know I will pass the class this year. As the days progress through towards the end of the month it is getting harder to get to class without being winded. I believed that I needed to do more exercising and build up my strength. I could not believe that my allergies could have been this bad. One week into the course and I just finished 6 of my online Pre-Algebra homework assignments finally. Have 6 more online assignments and 7 textbook assignments. Math is intense! I am determined that no matter how I feel that every morning I will get up and have a smile on my face and a positive attitude as my armor against the pain and breathing discomfort. I knew I could get through fall allergy season and in just a few days meet with the doctor and learn that I'm worrying about cancer for nothing. My mother taught me to get up, get moving and not worry. I need to remember the lessons she taught me and to stop taking the worry of the pain and discomfort of breathing as a problem. If I don't mind, it doesn't matter. I can do this!

I need to do it this way for me. I am not going to worry any longer on how everyone else will respond or react.

Chapter 4

My Battle Isn't Over

It has been four years since my initial cancer diagnosis and I'm going to get this new lump evaluated. I have an "I've been there and done that" feeling when I finally do head to my doctor's appointment. My daughter is safely back home to California. Jay is home to go to the doctor with me. Tonight he will go back to Miami for work. Today is nothing! It is just going to be more calcified scar tissue, just like every other time.

Dr. H. does his usual great exam. He decides to do an ultrasound to determine if additional tests are needed, he determines that it is a mass, not just calcification or scar tissue. He asks if I have any headaches.

"Yes," I tell him, "at the top right of my forehead, near my eye."

I have believed it was just from trying to adjust to new eye glasses. Never assume anything when you have had cancer in the past! Dr. H. writes a script for me to get a PET/CT scan and a brain MRI. It was scheduled for the following Friday. I'm extremely claustrophobic and need meds just to look at a PET/CT or MRI machine, so I must have Jay with me.

I don't think it has spread to my other breast, but we will know by the Monday after the tests. I expect that I will be needing to prepare to have the "mass" removed and then the usual round of chemotherapy and radiation if it truly is cancer. Doubt it, but anything is possible.

As I mentally prepare myself to have my MRI and PET/CT scans done, I turn to the computer and ask my friends that have battled cancer before "If you are a survivor, but get cancer again, what are you then?" I said that I believed that all survivors are always fighters and all fighters are survivors.

My response was that all survivors are fighters and all fighters are survivors. What do you think? The replies came flying in ranging from being a re-survivor and 2-time survivor to the extremely confident term of Super Survivor. Words, they can be very empowering

The online "world" is about to become a very important communication link between me and the world I know. I need to remember the Rule of Five, which is that you should do five things on a daily basis that will bring you closer to your goal. I decide to start with writing my thoughts and sharing what I can where I can.

My thoughts go to writing and trying to explain how I feel about the cancer. What does cancer think, if it could? How would it put words to the torment it does to our lives as we go through the process of the diagnosis and transition over to the treatment? The cancer is splitting cells inside me. It is with me everywhere, all the time.

I write the words. I express the glee that cancer would have as it permeated your entire body in a poem. I choose to call "I'm Inside of You".

I'm Inside of You

Every breath you take
Every move you make
Every twist and turn
Every lift and bend,
I'm inside of you.

Every time you sit,
Everywhere you stand,
Every smile you fake,
Every breath you take,
I'm inside of you.

22

Oh, Can't you see?!
I've merged with you
How my tendrils spread,
How I strengthen my grip,
With every breath you take.

You wish I was gone,
Lost without a trace!
You dream at night
Of the unblemished life.

You look around,
and it can't be found!
Those dreams you had,
That life you lived,
All mine now,
I'm inside of you.
You feel so cold and long
for a warm embrace
You keep crying, crying, please
Why did you choose me?
What did I do then?
What have I done now?

Oh can't you see ~

I'm inside of you.
Your body aches
With every breath you take.

Every move you make,
Every lift and bend
I'm inside of you!

So fake that smile
Dream of life again,
Just remember now,
It's all a dream,
I'm inside of you!

Chapter 5

The Waiting Game

Tomorrow I take a second step closer to my "fork-in-the-road" decision. Will I go with the high road or the low road? I have promised myself to have the necessary information to make that decision by the 17th of this month. The hardest part of making a decision is waiting on accurate information so that the correct decision can be made. That said, it is also a case of I'll make the best decision I can with the information available. Half of the information has been received and if based on that information alone I now know which road to take. If the information does not change significantly the decision has already been made. It will be time to fine tune the options and chose those that will be involved in the activities. Life is so much fun! Some days are a repeat of past days and others bring all new challenges and excitements.

Typical me, I'm a true Aries through and through. Then when you add in the Chinese Zodiac Sign, the Tiger, I barge my way through life and what I can't knock down I claw and chew to get out of my way. My roar has horns, teeth and claws. Laughing, I used to make decisions based on feeling (still do sometimes) not on evidence of information. I am trying to do better now that I'm older. Still waiting for information is not one of my strong points. I am still impatient and want things solved now, not in two or three weeks.

I'm asked if I am having more "drama" in my life. No, this isn't drama, this is real life. I have to make some choices and either way it will be easy to decide once I have enough information. Not only do I have to decide how to react and live with a potential diagnosis of cancer again, but I also need to consider a request to join two honor societies that I received at Hillsborough Community College. I need to also decide how much time I can spend doing those activities that will lead to future scholarships and still keep the G.P.A. I have. What point does planning for the long term future impact the short term present? Life is about balance and maintaining the balance can sometimes feel tricky.

I never tell anyone anything until after Jay and I have had an opportunity to discuss it. I know that those friends that are close to me will feel left out to some degree. However it is important that the decisions that need to be made are made by those that will be most impacted by them. First Jay and I, then our children. A diagnosis of cancer, if this is what it is, will change all of our lives and I must handle this with honesty, clarity and sensitivity. It would be insensitive to share partial information and cause unnecessary worry. I do not feel as if I can even share the worry with anyone but Jay at this time. Our children all have lives to live and many have families to raise. They can wait until we know more and have had a chance to decide how to best share it with them.

Part of being strong while dealing with difficult decisions is knowing that the ability to limit the knowledge that others have allows friends to be strong for you without even being aware that their normal behavior is a strength that you lean on during difficult times. Normal is by its very nature a resilient feature of friendship.

Chapter 6

Tests and Results

The day of my MRI and PET/CT scan finally arrives. It's been getting harder and harder to breathe. I'm beginning to think I might have more than just severe allergies this year. Still, I figure the worst thing the PET scan could come back with walking pneumonia. This diagnosis would just be antibiotics and I can still stay on track at school.

Some people don't understand what an MRI is. The formal name for an MRI is "Magnetic Resonance Imaging." It's a radiology technique used to visualize detailed internal structures in the human body. While that is the definition to the medical world, to me however an MRI means being trapped in a metal tube that closes in on me and threatens to collapse! Yep, total irrational fear. I already am dreading this appointment and my anxiety levels are increasing. Jay reminds me that I'll take my medication and nothing will bother me.

I know it's necessary. I know that it's time to put on my big girl shoes and let the world know I'm ready! My mask is on and I can proceed forward with the help of Valium! I don't mention the Valium part when I share information online. I will not show weakness today.

I share how excited I am. Jay is working from the home office today and we have our appointment during the afternoon with the surgeon. I'm glad that answers will be available or at least additional testing to find out what this lump is. It is such a wonderful day and the sun is shining.

I have worked hard to coordinate this plan of action. I shared with those that needed information, I let others continue on their journey of life so they could become all they deserved to be. I'm so happy that the events are moving smoothly. I appreciate seeing the sun reflecting off the gentle windblown waves on the lake behind the house. The water looks as if there are diamond dancing along the surface. This reminder of the beauty of nature refocuses me and prepares me for the afternoon.

A friend reminds me to keep allowing God to lead, guide and direct, to do all things through prayer and supplication. I don't think I have ever stopped allowing God to lead me. I might not always hear Him clearly and go the wrong way. I think everyone sometimes ceases to listen even for a short time. I told my friend, "Dang girl. He's driving this roller coaster called life!" Prayers have not stopped. I'm not bargaining, but I am relying on God for the support and strength. What is that about trials that make you strong?"

Much of what happened during the PET/CT and MRI is a fog. I do remember drinking the barium and receiving the injection of radioactive isotopes, taking my Valium and then getting into the PET/CT machine where I promptly fell asleep. I'm sure I was "aware" of the short walk from the trailer into Tower-Parsons for the MRI however I do not have an active memory of the activity. My next moment of awareness was when I was sitting in the car with Jay and checking the messages on my phone. How often does a doctor call and leave a message for you while you are still getting tests done?

Dr. H's message was something about having "Mets" and to please call him. When I call, I am to go over there. Easy enough. We drive over to his office parking lot, an entire two minutes away from the hospital parking lot and call his office. He explains that the PET/CT scan results showed metastases and a partially collapsed lung. I asked if I could see him in his office as I was in the parking lot. The surprise in his voice was evident as he told me to hurry inside.

Once Jay and I are inside the waiting room, we are quickly ushered to an examination room. Dr. H sticks his head in through the door and again states that the preliminary report shows "mets." He wants to look at it again to be sure and he'll be right back.

When the results findings for the Brain MRI arrive, they are less than ideal. The findings for the PET/CT scan are not what I had hoped for either.

The report for the scans showed multiple cancer lesions throughout my bones and in the lining between my right lung and the inner ribs and muscles.

BRAIN MRI REPORT FINDINGS

Multiple calvarial metastases are identified. The largest is a 13 mm metastasis in the left parietal region. Numerous other bilateral calvarial metastases are also noted. No abnormal brain or parenchymal signal is seen. There is no midline shift or focal mass effect present. There is normal differentiation of the gray and white matter. The ventricular system appears normal. The basal cisterns are patent. The brainstem and cerebellum are normal appearance. Normal flow voids present proximal intracranial arteries. No extra-axial fluid collections are seen. Post contrast images demonstrate presence of a venous angioma in the right frontal lobe. No other areas of abnormal enhancement are seen. No brain metastases identified. The visualized orbital structures and paranasal sinuses appear normal.

PET/CT SCAN REPORT FINDINGS

Postsurgical changes of right mastectomy are present. I do not see evidence of hypermetabolic activity involving the postsurgical right anterior chest wall. No hypermetabolic right axillary lymphadenopathy is detected. However, extensive metastatic disease is identified.

Hypermetabolic right hilar activity has a maximum SUV of 8.4. Right lung atelectasis is present with minimal aeration anteriorly. This is associated with a large right pleural effusion. There is mass effect with shift of the mediastinum to the left. Focal areas of hypermetabolic activity are identified along the pleura with a maximum SUV of 7.7.

Right internal mammary hypermetabolic lymphadenopathy is

present. One of these measures 2.4 cm with a maximum SUV of 11.0. Smaller right internal mammary hypermetabolic lymph nodes have a maximum SUV of 8.0

Extensive diffuse osseous metastases are also present. These involve the spine, ribs, pelvis and shoulders. At L1, the posterior cortex of the vertebral body is destroyed and there may be spinal canal involvement.
Small right adnexal mass does not appear hypermetabolic. I suspect this is an adnexal cyst.

Dr. H was notified of the above findings by telephone on 09/10/2010

Okay, fine, I think. So the chest lump is called "Mets." We'll just cut all the Mets out and get on with living. My biggest concern is how to reflate the lung. That just might hurt. The only thing that's truly concerning is the look on his face. Dr. H looks like his world just fell down. I did not realize that he very rarely has to tell a patient that they have Metastatic Disease or terminal cancer. It was hard for him to explain what Mets meant in my case. I have extensive cancer spread into my chest, skull, ribs, pelvis, shoulders and spine. This news is devastating for Dr. H. I truly did not yet understand the seriousness of the diagnosis. It takes several weeks for me to get a decent understanding of what mets are and how they will affect my life. For now, the lack of knowledge is a great benefit to my mental outlook and ability to make decisions.

The doctor is back. It appears that the lung is a bigger issue than I thought. He wants me to check into the hospital right now. Mets means that my cancer has spread to other areas, and the lung is filling with fluid and could get worse.

Jay and I disagree. We have decided that this weekend is going to be a fun weekend for us. I have plans to get my haircut, go out to dinner and other family fun.

I finally decided that I'll check in Monday as a compromise to what my doctor was requesting. He makes me promise to check in earlier if my breathing becomes more compromised. Heck, it's only 60 percent reduced at this moment. I can make it until Monday!

It's the end of the day. We've made some phone calls to daughters and sisters to let them know what happened today. Everyone is so very supportive. Now I will tell my online friends that Monday I get admitted to the hospital, but I will be doing a haircut and donate my hair first! I am not prepared for what my friends will say. I know there is going to be sorrow and grief and lots of "Oh no!" comments, but I know that I will be able to lean on many of them.

"The decision has been made," I shared. "The choice is tough to live with, deadly not to make. I am ready to fight. Metastatic Breast Cancer. It is in my ribs, hips, shoulders, and possibly my spine. I also have 60 percent lung capacity. I will be admitted to hospital on Monday for lung surgery and chemo. Off to dinner with family to enjoy a sunset! The fight is on! Haircut tomorrow!"

"Love you mom! You'll beat it this time too!" My daughter responds.

"Let's all cut our hair and wear Kewl hats. What should we put on the hats? It doesn't look like it in my pic, but I still have a lot of hair to cut. FWIW My cousin Barb, God Love her, she went 15 years with a similar diagnosis. She had many years watching her children's weddings and the arrival of Grandbabies."

I treasure all of my friends and their prayers. A friend offers all her love, as well as her "guardian angel sister" to fight at my side.

I keep my update as positive as possible, while not sugar-coating the truth: "My prognosis is dire. However with aggressive treatment I will survive. My surgeon is treating a patient with same diagnosis for the last 7 years. I'll be at Brandon Hospital Monday! They need to drain fluid around lung and re-inflate the lung. Then start chemo. Laptop, books, cellphones, I'll be all set!"

I know that I am on the right track when another friend encourages me to keep that positive attitude--it worked for her. She is a stage 4

31

breast cancer survivor of twelve years. If she can do it, I can do it.

"That is why we walk the Three Day," she posts. "I will keep you in my prayers."

I'm reminded that I'm a strong lady with a lot of supportive friends and loved ones. With the support of the other "pink warriors" and other friends, we know we will win this battle. They have no doubt and I can't afford to doubt.

My support system keeps the prayers and positive vibes coming my way. Offers of help and of home visits start to roll in. A friend shares, "When God looks at you, He sees a woman who is beautifully perfect and perfectly beautiful, a survivor whose strength has led her through adversity, a kind and generous spirit who makes the world a gentler place, a reflection of His own love and light. See yourself as God sees you. I am so sorry Karen. My deepest prayers for you and your family. I wish I could do more, but all I know is to keep walking till we find your cure. Hope and ((HUGS)) my friend." Another offers of a candle being lit at every church service that particular friend attends until I "get through this." Certainly they all understand that Stage 4 with Mets means that it will never be gotten through? Or do they mean through this particular event? My friends are still talking about winning battles and finding "my cure." There is "no cure" for metastatic disease. I will sooner or later, and I'd rather later, die from this. But until then I must find a purpose and live.

In his book *"The Purpose Driven Life"*, Rick Warren writes:

"Hope is as essential to your life as air and water. You need hope to cope. Dr. Bernie Siegel found he could predict which of his cancer patients would go into remission by asking, "Do you want to live to be a hundred?" Those with a deep sense of purpose answered . . . yes and were the ones most likely to survive. Hope comes from having a purpose. If you have felt hopeless, hold on! Wonderful changes are going to happen in your life as you begin to live it on purpose."

I have to have a purpose-driven life. God has promised me he has good plans for me, not plans for pain. He will give me hope and a good future. Only God knows what is going to happen and we can only pray, continue to fight, and keep the faith.

Not everyone is ready to be supportive, of course. Not everyone knew of my diagnosis before I posted it. I find myself in the position of needing to comfort them for what is happening to me. I respond to their tears and their need to hear my voice as they battle with the unfairness of what is happening to me, to all of us.

My oldest daughter shares with her friends the emotional impact this has for her. "Just had my entire world turned upside down. Damn I wish I wasn't alone right now. Its stage 4 breast cancer. In her hips, ribs, shoulders and possibly spine. Lung capacity 60 percent. Surgery and chemo on Monday. Please pray for my mom."

Even in her fear and grief she was able to project a positive supportive non-fearful attitude during the telephone call. She has been one of my many pillars of strength. I did not consider before I decided to support her decision to move how my potential diagnosis would impact her, alone, in California. Friends and in-laws are not the same thing as family. I wondered if I had done her a disservice by not allowing her to be involved in the potential issues beforehand. Would she forgive me?

My fourth daughter admitted to crying at the news. "Mom--just keep in mind, that like your first run in with this issue, I was there whenever you needed me, and even though I am a few more hours away than last time, all I need is a two day heads up and I can be right down there. We all know you will fight this battle and win. Remember, there are so many people standing next to you in support. Stay strong, don't cry as much as me and keep us updated."

My youngest daughter reaches out to her friends. She says "My mom has stage 4 cancer. Please keep her in your prayers if you are religious. This is going to be a hard time for our family."

I had no concept of just how hard it was about to become.

Chapter 7

Fight or Flight

Friends, both those I have a personal connection with and those I only have a computer connection with, are all rallying to support me with positive thoughts and prayers. This time it's not just Jay and me against the cancer. We both will have help and support. Many people don't think of just how much support the spouse or caregiver truly needs during the diagnosis and treatments.

Today a friend shared about my diagnosis:

"Another friend has heard that awful C-word again today. Stage 4 metastatic breast cancer. In her hips, ribs, shoulders and possibly spine. Lung capacity 60 percent. Surgery and chemo on Monday. Please pray for Karen Lewandowski. Just one more reason I am fighting to find a cure for this disease. I am so sick of cancer."

It stuns me that she, as well as many others, are nearly as devastated as my daughters were. We walked together in the last three-day walk in our community, Barefoot Diva teammates. I wonder if I will ever be healthy enough to walk sixty miles over a three-day period again. It was great to be part of the team. However, right now I must concentrate on what needs to be done today and not worry about the future.

My sisters contact me. While I am the oldest of the children, my next oldest sister has been a source of constant support in my life.

"Remember sis, you are a breast cancer survivor first, a patient second. I love you so much, I will be seeing you soon. At the latest only four more months, get better soon. We have a cruise to go on next year! My treat you know."

I have no intention of not being around for this cruise! I can't wait to connect with my sisters.

My very youngest sister also posted right after with more words of encouragement. "I couldn't have said it better, and I fully agree with her you are a survivor first!"

Sometimes however, you have to be a warrior while you are surviving or you cease to survive. I wonder how to explain that to my sisters?

Would anyone ever understand the difference in the mental process of separating fighting over just "surviving"? It's like the instinctive fight or flight behaviors of animals. I can chose flight by only surviving, or I can stand up and fight back.

Chapter 8

Power Control

I woke up this morning, Saturday, September 11, 2010. It's hard to believe that I am going to get my haircut, and may be facing chemo again. It's hard to believe that I have cancer again. Mets, when you don't know what the word means it doesn't make it as scary. Cancer is not something to be afraid of. All it is, is a few rampant cells that have decided to morph their positions, change your DNA structure, and try to kill you.

Cancer doesn't have Power. Cancer can't change your happiness. Cancer can't stop the smiles. Cancer can't make you angry. Cancer truly has no power unless you give it power. I'm not giving any of my power away!

I turn on the computer and go online. I have lots of things to do today but I want to see how my friends are reacting. The first post I see is from a local favorite three-day walker. He posted a photograph of himself and my standard poodle for his comment. He captioned it, "Thor, of the famous 'Karen and Thor.' Love you Karen, my angel. Hope you are feeling nice and warm, your heart is as close to my heart as I can get you." Both the picture and the comment made me smile, lightening the day's load just a little bit. Thor is my service dog, a standard poodle. We have walked several 60 mile 3 day walks together to raise funds and awareness for early detection of breast cancer. To find a cure to prevent others from getting breast cancer.

I finally responded to my daughter, Kristina, about being there when I needed her. I responded "I love you Princess. Right now I need to get through surgery and then on to chemo. I love you!" I tried to remind her that she was not alone and her son was there with her. I did not want her to block him out in her grief.

I shared with my friends and family online that I had gone off my healthy diet the night before. I actually had a Long Island iced tea with dinner at Little Harbor and then I slept like a rock! Okay, well, do rocks really sleep? I did sleep for six hours and woke up truly awake and ready for the new day. Sunset at Little Harbor is beautiful from inside the restaurant.

Another cancer survivor told me that I deserved to have an entire pitcher of Long Island Ice Tea. The one comment about my drink leads to others in support of my tiny rebellion, including one that suggested that some of us get together for a "tea" party once I am released from the hospital. I'm surprised nobody has hit me over the head for holding out on what was happening until I had answers to give. Even my daughters are not upset about that.

I replied, "However, I did sleep like a baby for six hours. My health coach is a former Mr. USA in the body building world. He has been helping me live a more fit and healthy lifestyle. I will have to find out how to make hospital food healthy!"

While I was commenting about falling off my diet, my health lifestyle coach, Former Mr. USA, was looking for a graphic to tag on my page. The photograph he posted on my page shows a pair of strong male hands clasped together in prayer, resting on the pages of an open Bible. The impact I had had on people before I knew my cancer came back and the degree with which they are showing they care strengthens me, supports me, and amazes me. He posted on his page, "Urgent. Please pray for healing. I ask all of my friends to pray for our friend Karen."

The thought of the multitude of prayers starting, for me, was humbling. The date was not lost on me. Shouldn't this date stay in my memory of the events in New York, Washington DC and in that empty field in Pennsylvania? But that was impossible. That day will forever share the memory of my telling all my friends that I have stage IV cancer. It will forever share the support and the strength that my friends and total strangers gave to me.

37

My plans for the day are simple. I'm going to get my haircut. I'm not sure where yet. I have to make some phone calls see who can get me in today. Apollo Beach is a small town. Appointments for haircuts fill up two weeks in advance. If I had known two weeks ago I would be going into the hospital Monday, it would have been easier to find a hairdresser's chair to sit in. Tomorrow, Sunday, I am going to join some friends and get photographed with a pair of pink boxing gloves during a photo shoot for "Fight Like a Girl." I'm really looking forward to this exciting opportunity!

Of course, the day after tomorrow is Monday. That's the day I get to go to the hospital, where a thoracic surgeon is going to drain the fluid from around my right lung. From what I understand, he will leave at least one drain in place so that any remaining fluid will come out. Since I have mets I expect to be doing the chemotherapy and radiation routine again. As much as I disliked my port last time I can deal with another one for a few short weeks. The port will make the infusion for the chemotherapy faster and more efficient, as well as less dangerous.

I share a summary of this information on Facebook. A friend finds a stylist who will cut my hair for me. We've agreed to give the hair to an organization called Locks of Love. Many of my friends now know that the cancer is back. I see it mentioned in the positive comments that continue the prayers.

One of the gals wrote "Remember, bald is so much easier to care for! Best of luck to you and make God guide the surgeon's hands."

She is right, bald is beautiful and it really is so much easier to care for. Just slap a little soap on your head, wash it with the washcloth, and rinse it off. Shower time cut 75 percent.

More comments supporting the bald look are similar to this one:

"Karen, keep smiling girlfriend. We are all keeping our prayers going your way. Think of this as a stepping stone in life. Attitude is everything. And yes, honey, bald is beautiful and it makes getting ready in the morning a breeze."

Speed bumps, molehills, mountains. At what point does a speed bump become a mountain? At what point can we take a mountain and make it a molehill? It's all about attitude. I will have a great attitude. I've played this game before. There's nothing that can keep me down.

I am dawdling. It is time to get some breakfast, to get in the shower and go get that fantastic new haircut. It's only when I try to achieve these things that I admit to being an overachiever. I keep thinking I can do everything I need to do and handle it all, all by myself. There are so many things I have to do and just want to do. I keep telling myself I can manage all of them, when the truth of the matter is that just trying to take a shower has left me exhausted. When I come out of the shower, it's hard just to breathe. I need to lie down.

Reality begins to set in. If just taking a shower makes me just tired, I have a feeling that tomorrow's plans are going to be greatly different than what I had anticipated.

My former 3-day walk team captain just called. She was able to get in touch with one of her friends who is a hair stylist. I have an appointment to have my hair cut and the hair will be sent off to Locks of Love in my name. Time to get moving and headed out of the house. Jay, Tina and I discuss how short I should cut my hair in preparation for the upcoming treatments.

Upon arriving at the salon I get my hair put into a ponytail. The 13 inches of hair is slowly cut off. During my haircut, we remove about twelve to thirteen inches of hair. I still have some hair left, despite taking so much off. This new haircut is short, sassy, and nicely layered. Everyone says it looks cute. My head feels lighter, as if somebody removed eight pounds from it. I know my hair did not weigh that much. How long before start missing my hair?

There is a truism that says a woman's hair is her crowning glory. My hair is much more than my crowning glory. My long hair symbolizes my beating cancer. My short hair, this new cute style that barely brushes the back of my collar, marks not beating cancer. This new hair style also symbolizes the new strength of the woman. This woman has become a warrior! She is armed, ready, and as far as the cancer's concerned, she is dangerous.

My friend has gone to pick up my ponytails and package them to mail to Locks of Love. She tells me that, for her, the task is a bittersweet one. Her heart aches for me and for what they represent, but then she comments, "How great it is for you to be able to give something of yourself, even while your body is being brutally attacked by cancer."

For me, giving my hair away to Locks of Love was not so much about giving away part of me, as it is about sharing the strength and the courage I have with others. I knew I was going to fight with everything I had. Now they, these unknown others, have the hair that marks my being a survivor. I hope those hairs I sent, each individual strand, is put into many different hairpieces. I hope the strength of my being a survivor carries through those hairpieces, and into the beings of those others who receive that hair. I wish them strength, courage, and the ability to tackle everything, in spite of any odds that might be put before them.

Just the trip out to get the haircut has caused me to be tired again. We all agree to have lunch and then home for a nap. I will wait until Monday to go to the hospital. I do not want my weekend to be interrupted by cancer. Tomorrow will be the photo shoot with the other cancer survivors.

I'm sitting here giggling and laughing, until I cough and cry. Laughing hurts. I don't know when I can laugh again, but I truly hope that someday I'll be able to laugh without coughing and without pain. I'm laughing because, guess what, I have a brain and amazingly I even have a heart. I can prove it. I've taken some time before dinner to sit here with my laptop and I'm looking at the films from the PET scan and the MRI. It shows where the Mets might be and the disk in my spine that is collapsing. It shows I have a heart. I finally found it, even when my daughters didn't believe I had a heart!

So much is going on today. If I don't have to end up at the hospital early, like tomorrow, I need to take it easy. It is time to go to bed, I send my daughters a message wishing them a good night.

Chapter 9

Butterfly Kisses and Coffee

"Good morning! Don't ask me to exert myself and I'll visit online with you as long as you like today. Tomorrow is hospital check-in day! I've already had my gentle wake up this morning."

It is September 12, 2010. I wake up to the feel of soft kisses brushing my cheek and a gentle caress of the hand on my new short hair.

"Good morning beautiful it's time to wake up."

Fresh coffee awaited me. Walking to the dining room table, two simple rooms away, was more difficult today than yesterday. I felt as if I were gasping for breath.

I'm not worse. I am not going into the hospital today! I have put my feet up and, pulled my laptop onto my lap. After all, isn't that where laptop belongs is in the lap? It's time to talk to my family online. It's time to talk with my friends through email. It is not time to talk on the telephone. It seems like I can do two things at once now, I can breathe and walk or I can walk and talk. Simple solution. I'm not talking.

I can't figure out why my right lung hurts more when I use my left arm, doesn't hurt to use my right arm. I am doing pretty darn well. The hurt—yes it hurts! I won't downplay that. But it's part of the adventure that God has set before me. Many years ago I told him cancer was His problem. My cancer it still belongs to Him. I'm only sick, I only truly have cancer, on the days I see the doctor. That limitation, that rule, includes the time I spend in the hospital.

No, let's make it even better that: the hospital is like a vacation. It's a place in which the doctors are giving me the chance to relax from school for a few days. I'll give them those days. I'm only sick when the doctor is in the room. This time, now and in the hospital, is a time to rejoice in these challenges and the new things I know I will learn. Yes, I'd love a miracle. I'd love complete remission. But if complete remission is not to be, then I am here for the journey and I will be blazing a trail.

I spend the afternoon learning about pleural effusion and how it is a complication of breast cancer. I want to get the healing on the fast track. I want to get back to school. I've already missed one day of intermediate algebra. As it is, I am going to miss at least two more days of school. I want and need to be in school. I have goals. Cancer will not stop me from meeting my goals.

When I wake from my nap, I see that a friend has shared his experience today by posting; "My friends who have cancer. When one might ask 'why?' You have answered 'because I can make it beautiful.' It was an amazing photo shoot today, with Fight like a Girl, but don't be fooled, it's not about the picture, it's about the subject. I was honored to stand with some of the subjects. It's a crazy surreal life in which I live, thank you to all those that let me share it with them."

I so missed going. I had my heart set on going to the shoot. I wanted to stand beside other survivors and warriors, to stand beside those who inspire, to stand together. I wanted to show that we are stronger than cancer. Instead, cancer is stronger at this moment than I want it to be. This photo shoot, it's gone. It's over. It will never be recreated, repeated, or redone. I will never have this opportunity again. Damn cancer for stealing a moment!

The outpouring of care and concern hasn't slowed down. The emails continue unceasingly. If at any point I feel I can't be strong for myself or I can't be strong for my family, my friends are giving me their strength so I can make it one moment more. One moment. That's all it takes. Just another moment to be. My grandsons in California put my name on the prayer list of their church today. They and their mother, my oldest daughter, are praying for me. They have faith I will beat this disease and recover in no time.

I have no tears, not now. I will not shed tears, I will not give in to my fear. Cancer it is not worthy of my tears. A strong person knows how to keep their life in order. Even when they have tears in their eyes, they still managed to say I'm okay. I am okay. I might have tears when they puncture through my skin and the push the catheter into my lung lining and into the inner membrane to drain the fluid that built up and now is compressing my lung. Then I might cry. I have prayed and others have prayed that I will have the strength and courage to meet this challenge head-on. Knowing that I can cry, but more importantly knowing that I can be strong, is what will make me a survivor.

In the morning, we are going to leave for the hospital in Brandon after my sister goes to school. I can't wait! I really should go today.

Chapter 10

The New Journey Begins

Jay gets up at his normal time. He makes sure my sister is awake and up, that she has breakfast and gets off to school. Before she leaves to catch the school bus, my sister comes in to say "good morning" and that she will see me later. I take a shower and get dressed, while Jay takes care of the dogs. Each step I take slowly, it truly has gotten harder to breathe. Maybe I should have done this last Friday.

We pack for a short trip to the hospital. Pack? I guess that is what you consider it. I took my algebra book, my algebra notes, my homework, my laptop, assorted pens, pencils and erasers, and a few books to read. I am ready.

No, I have to take clothes also. Clothes, really? I'm just going to get some fluid drained off my lung. I don't expect that I'll be in the hospital for more than a day or two. I certainly won't be there for a week or longer.

Moon dust. Jay's car makes me smile because of the name of its color. The GMC Trailblazer is very comfortable to ride in. I can recline my seat back and relax for the drive. Jay opens the door and helps me sit down. He grasps my seat belt and reaches across me, securely snaps it in place and pulls it snug against my hips. Giving me a quick and gentle kiss on the cheek. Jay pats me on the leg. I can hear his smile in his voice as he tells me I'm safe. I begin to recline my seat. Almost as quickly, I stop instantly. The seatback comes upright, completely vertical. I smile and match it in my eyes. I pray that this ride will be the shortest ride to town we have ever taken.

Jay slowly backs up the car. Jay navigates out of the neighborhood, checking carefully for children. We pass the elementary students at the bus stop. Jay seems to know instinctively how uncomfortable this ride is. The right turn is deliberate, gradual.

Our conversation is equally deliberate. We talk about pleural effusion. We have both researched it. It is a simple thing, fluid that has collected in the very microscopically small space between the two linings of my lung. Most people don't think about how they inhale air into their lungs or how the ribs move out and the diaphragm moves down. Breathing just IS. They don't think about how, when the lungs expand, this lining has to move and slide with every chest wall movement. What allows this slippery, sliding movement is the pleural lining of your lung. A very small amount of fluid lubricates these two surfaces preventing chafing and irritation. When too much fluid accumulates between those surfaces, like in my lung, the lungs can no longer expand or move, and breathing becomes difficult.

We come to the traffic light at Shell Point Road. This intersection has limited visibility. On the best of days, even with the green light and the clearest of visibility, drivers still slow down for the corner. Jay turns the turn signal indicator on, click, click – click, click – click, click. The familiar sounds are comforting. He takes the turn 5 mph, a wide, sweeping, gentle turn.

I scream!

I frantically reach over the passenger window for the hand bar. I use my left hand to brace and push my body up. I'm crying, not gentle soft flowing tears that are cleansing and healing, but tears of agony and pain. My back has never hurt like this.

"Why did you go so fast?" I ask him.

Jay's grieved expression stops me in my place. He tells me how slow he went around the corner, how he took it wide. He promises to be more careful with the next ones.

If he was so careful, why is it so painful? What is going on with my back?

The hospital is about twenty miles away. We pass the elementary school. Mothers and fathers are dropping off their children. We see children walking in small groups on the sidewalk, talking and smiling. It's a typical fall day in Florida. You won't see any sweaters or jackets today.

We drive past all the businesses approaching the interstate. The cloverleaf is going to be interesting. I am still in tears from the turn. Typically these types of entrance ramps are my favorite, I brace myself to the back of the seat and I accelerate to the most that I can and fly through them. But not today!

"Please," I say to Jay, "slow down for the entrance ramp?"

As we drive north on the interstate, I see the trees on the berm, tall, green and thick. The river is just over the rise. Dolphins and manatees are known to inhabit this river. Today, there is no pleasure in gazing at the river.

I cry throughout the entire drive, holding onto the grab bar and the passenger door as I try hard to prevent my back from swaying to the left or the right. The pain from this ride hurts worse than when I climbed out of the kayak, or when I squatted down trying to get a key into a lock. It finally sinks in. Mets. It means pain. This pain is what I will have to face for the rest my life. Can I just suck it up? Where will I find the strength to live with this type of pain every day? Can I do it?

We arrive at the hospital and walk to the main entrance to check in. My breast surgeon could not schedule us to check in. We have to walk around to the emergency room. Once there I am processed through triage, where they evaluate me to determine how urgent my care needs to be. From that point forward, time flies in the emergency room. I'm lying on a hospital bed. The pulmonologist is there and we're discussing the options for draining my lung. It will require surgery, which can't be done until at least tomorrow. However, if the pain is so unbearable, he'll go ahead to numb my skin and pop a quick drain in to remove some of the pressure.

"Will I be awake for this procedure or asleep?" I ask.

The pulmonologist explains that putting a tube in is just a temporary procedure. I would not be anesthetized. I will wait, I cannot imagine the needle piercing my skin and going into my lung without complete anesthesia. I am admitted to the hospital and scheduled to go to my room. The new journey begins.

Chapter 11

Diagnoses are Made

I am admitted to the hospital and I am checked into my room. My back hurts! I am offered pain medication and do not turn it down. I don't fully realize the degree or the speed with which my memories and ability to make decisions will rapidly disappear with the acceptance of the medication. In retrospect, I am glad that we went to the effort to have Jay made my medical advocate and had a lawyer do the medical power of attorney for us. Jay will have a lot of decisions to make with me. I don't want to make the wrong decision. This decision is about my life, we must do it right.

Day one is just simply a day of intake, medication and rest. The medical team here at the hospital has had an opportunity to evaluate my condition. Reports start flowing in.

ATTENDING PHYSICIAN: AHF, MD

HISTORY: This is a very pleasant 48-year old female, very unfortunate, with a past medical history significant for breast cancer diagnosed in year 2006 status post chemotherapy and right-sided mastectomy. The patient has been suffering from right-sided chest wall pain for the past 1 week. The patient stated that it felt like a lump under the right side of the chest area. The patient was seen by her surgeon, Dr. JMH, and underwent a PET scan and MRI of the brain.

She was told there was an abnormal uptake to the ribs, shoulders, hip as well as L1 and also noted to have a significant right-sided pleural effusion. The patient was unable to tolerate the pain and spasm anymore and she presented herself today to

48

the ER where she was evaluated and was recommended to be admitted for further management.

EKG has been requested. Chest x-ray reveals a large right pleural effusion. CT angio of the chest reveals no evidence of pulmonary embolism, large right pleural effusion with compressive atelectasis involving the right middle lobe and right lower lobe is noted.

PLAN: Admit the patient to medical floor. Surgical consultation with Dr. H as well as Dr. FK noted and appreciated. The patient will require to go under pleurodesis. We will monitor the patient postop closely. Meanwhile the patient will be placed on IV antibiotics including Maxipime and Zithromax. Discharge plan depending on further workup once the patient's condition is improved and once pleural effusion is resolved.

CONSULTING PHYSICIAN: JMH, MD

ASSESSMENT/PLAN: Stage IV breast cancer. She will require multimodiality therapy. Cardiothoracic surgeon will need to do a thoracoscopy drainage and pleurodesis with cytology of the fluid. I have also consulted Hematology/Oncology and Radiation Oncology for I believe that patient obviously will need salvage chemotherapy and radiation therapy. At this point, the diagnosis in my eyes is grave but of course we will be very optimistic and push and help in any way we can.

CONSULTING PHYSICIAN: FBK, MD

PLAN: I discussed all of the findings with the patient, explained to her that I can arrange for an ultrasound-guided thoracentesis and then plan for a thoracoscopy, drainage of fluid and possible pleurodesis but she said that she is comfortable on 2L nasal cannula and only having discomfort and she has severe muscle spasm on the back, so she would not like to have a thoracentesis done rather would go for

49

thoracoscopy and drainage of the fluid, explained to her that at any time she becomes short of breath. Then in that case, we have to put a chest tube in her. She fully understands and wished to proceed in the morning for the procedure. I discussed the procedure with her and her husband, explained to them the procedure the risks, benefits and complications associated with the procedure. I answered all of their questions and concerns with full satisfaction. They fully understand, they wished to proceed and aware that at any time her respiratory status become more unstable, she will then have to place a chest tube.

CLINICAL REPORT:

Pain was controlled by morphine, robaxin and valium. I spoke with Dr. AHF who will admit. Patient counseled in person regarding the patient's condition, test results and diagnosis. Old ED and inpatient records reviewed.

DISPOSITION: Admitted

CONDITION: Fair

FINDINGS: Large pleural effusion opacifying the lower two thirds of the right hemithorax with trace effusion extending to the apex. Left lung is clear. Mild leftward mediastinal shift.

CLINICAL IMPRESSION: Dyspnea, Pleural effusion, Breast cancer – female. Metastases present.

All these reports say essentially the same thing. I am having difficulty breathing and require additional oxygen to remain stable until tomorrow, when I can have the thoracoscopy and drain the fluid. Right now, I am on antibiotics tonight and breathing treatments. I post my first day update. I have already asked my daughters to log in as needed and help keep everyone updated. Between Jay, the girls and I, communication will be a breeze.

The thoracic surgeon is the first to arrive. He spends some time with Jay and me, explaining the procedure and our options. He gave me a choice, which is not always a great idea. I could choose to have a baby fine needle prick into my lung and they could suction some fluid this afternoon. This option is a non-sedated procedure, during which they use ultrasound to implant a drain tube to reduce the fluid level until they can get me into surgery. Or I could choose to have no procedure today at all.

I have chosen to not have any procedure today and will wait for tomorrow. Tomorrow's surgery will be done while I'm under anesthesia. During surgery, they will put a tube in my chest to remove any fluid and seal the lung to the pericardial sac with talc. He will also insert a tube down my throat to check and biopsy my lungs to see if the cancer has spread there. In three days the tube will be removed.

I explain that I am comfortable on the 2 liters of oxygen. I'm not interested in two procedures when a single one will work just fine. Why would anyone choose to do a one-day procedure over the course of two days?

Next to arrive was my breast surgeon. He spent about twenty minutes discussing what he would like to see in my treatment plan: fluid removed from chest, chemotherapy, radiation therapy, menu changes. He does not want me to implement any exercise program. This plan sounds like another year-long journey with doctors.

Finally the oncologist arrives. A possibility exists that the fluid is a result of an infection. Until the infection is cleared I will be unable to receive any chemotherapy treatments. After the chest is addressed and I'm released to home, I'm to force food and limit fluids. For the current time I'm only allowed liquids when I eat meals.

That's the treatment plan to feel healthy. Currently I'm only short of breath and frustrated with the muscle spasm that I now know is cancer pain.

The chemotherapy doctor did say that for the next several days he expects that I will not want to eat because of the chest pain. I must believe that God will give me the strength to eat in spite of the chest surgery and any pain. I'm going to finish the food on my tray and get ready to sleep. I bid everyone online a safe night and tell them to watch for tomorrow's update when I wake up from my medically-

51

induced nap.

Good night, hug your loved ones and tell them how important they are to you.

I am falling asleep and still need to decide if I'm brave enough to get out of bed to do something called a "urine analysis deposit" for the nurse. Moving and walking hurts, I'm unsure if I'm up to this yet.

The replies flood in while I am asleep. It is wonderful to wake up to such support. They wish me the best of luck, as well as prayers. They praise my strength, telling me that I am stronger than cancer, that I am a true Pink Warrior. Someone writes, "Wish I could be there to hold your hand through this but you'd probably end up supporting me more than vice versa. You are so brave, I know you will get thru this fine." My sister reminds me that she always has and always will love me dearly, telling me that she can't wait to see me next year. We're going to have so much fun, just us girls!

Visitors, I am told I had them. I, sadly, have no real memory of what happened during their visit. I was so happy to see them when they were there. Visitors encourage and share strength when they visit. I am very sorry at the time that I did not have the strength to visit for as long as they would have like and that I am unable to remember the details of their visits. The not remembering is disturbing, but I need to let that go and focus on getting healthy. My friends and family understand that the medication has side effects I can't control.

I'm being treated not only for the pleural effusion, but also for respiratory illness. I'm on antibiotics and Zithromax. All these medications and the pain medications for my back are making me so tired. The last post I see is from my sister. She said, "Karen, hugs to you my dear sister. You are very important to me! Close your eyes and wrap your arms around yourself, do you feel that? It's my long distance hug! I love you! You are my pink warrior!"

Tonight I shall close my eyes and imagine the hug from my sister. I am looking forward to her arriving here in Florida next year.

When I awake, I am on a nothing by mouth diet. The meds still flow into my IV drip line. My sister provided a very good description of my lung condition to my newsfeed and I no longer worry about having to explain what is going to happen to me for the friends who are following me on social media.

My back still hurts. Pain medications are not managing the pain. I feel loopy and disjointed. Today is the day my chest surgery will be performed. I am waiting for the operating room to be ready. My decision to wait until Monday to go to the hospital has resulted in the complete collapse of my right lung. Did I make a mistake? Was being stubborn and insistent the right decision?

I fall asleep and when I wake I am back in my room. My friends online have been filling up my page today. Before surgery there is a post that is on my timeline:

"Sometimes life throws us curves. We could stand there, take them and let strikes build against us till we strike out. But we don't do that. We swing away and turn those strikes into hits. So keep swinging, Karen, fight the adversity in your life, and hit that home run. We are all on your team cheering you on. You will win this battle. All the best wishes."

It is obvious that my daughters are going to become the key communicators on my page during this time. I am very blessed to have them and that they are willing to keep my friends and my family informed.

One of my daughters posts, "Mom is waiting for surgery still. When it is over she will be recovering in the ICU which is normal. We will update as we get them."

Another daughter posts, "Okay! Mom would like a prayer chain started. Please everybody, keep her in your thoughts and pray for her. As big of a prayer chain we can get, the better!"

My younger daughter follows up, saying, "Time to rally. Let's all get the prayers going for mom! Mom is on her way to surgery. Dr. estimates an hour to an hour and a half before the next update. Let's strengthen this prayer chain!"

My friends are told that I am out of surgery and in the recovery room. It feels like a very long time before I am assigned to a private room.

The surgeon, Dr. FBK noted in his report how the procedure was done. I am unsurprised to learn the lung had completely collapsed. I am, however, surprised that the cancer was what caused the pleural effusion. I will never take the simple act of breathing for granted again.

DESCRIPTION OF PROCEDURE: The patient was placed in the operating room table in supine position and under general endotracheal anesthesia, fiberoptic bronchoscopy was performed. There was no abnormality detected in the trachea and below the endotracheal tube. There was no extrinsic compression or intraluminal masses was noticed. Then, the right mid and right mainstem bronchus was cannulated and through the right upper lobe, bronchus intermedius, middle lobe and lower lobe were individually cannulated and examined to the subsegmental level. There was no intraluminal mass, but there was extrinsic compression causing about 30 percent to 40 percent collapse of the middle lobe and the lower lobe bronchus and there was copious amount of thick white mucusy secretions, which were aspirated. Then, the left mainstem bronchus was cannulated and through that the left upper lobe and the left lower lobe were individually cannulated and examined to the subsegmental level. There was no evidence of any intraluminal mass, any extrinsic compression, any atelectasis or collapse was noticed. Then, the patient had a double-lumen endotracheal tube placed. She was placed in the left lateral decubitus position with the right chest up. The entire right chest was prepped and draped in a regular sterile fashion. A small incision was made in the mid axillary line, in the fifth intercostal space and through that dissection was carried and a 5-mm trocar cannula was placed in the chest cavity and then thorascope was advanced. It was noticed that the entire parietal mediastinal pleura and the diaphragmatic pleura was studded with multiple masses all over the parietal pleura and there was large pleural effusion, which was causing completely collapse of the lung. Then under direct visualization, another 5-mm trocar cannula was placed in the fifth intercostal space along the mid and anterior midclavicular line and through that a 5-mm trocar cannula was placed. Then, a suction was replaced through that trocar and about 1800 cc of serosanguineous fluid was aspirated and that fluid was sent to pathology for cytology. Then, the direct visualization with the help of a grasper, multiple masses on the parietal pleura, they were biopsied and sent to pathology. Then, through a separate incision, a 24-French chest tube was placed and was secured to the skin using 0 silk suture. After that, under direct visualization, talc pleurodesis was done. The talc was sprayed over the visceral pleura, parietal pleura, diaphragmatic pleura and the mediastinal pleura and then the clamp was removed from the lung and the lung was allowed to inflate. After that, once the lung was fully inflated, then the trocar cannulas were removed. The subcutaneous tissue in the muscle were approximated using 2-1 Vicryl in the figure-of-eight fashion and the skin was closed using 4-0 Monocryl in subcuticular fashion. The operative area was cleaned, dried, and the dressing was placed. The chest tube was attached to the Pleur-evac. The patient tolerated the procedure well without any problems. She was extubated in the operating room and was transferred to the recovery room in stable condition for further monitoring.

The biopsies came back with rare atypical cells, mesothelial cells and lymphocytes from the right pleural fluid. The atypical cells probably represent reactive mesothelial cells. I am concerned that reactive mesothelial cells mean a new kind of cancer, but I have been assured that they are seen when there is an infection or inflammatory process underway. The biopsies of the masses on the parietal pleura were not as good as that of the fluid that had been drained. Those biopsies come back supporting a diagnosis of metastatic carcinoma possible of breast origin. Additional tests are going to be conducted on those masses and additional reports will be forthcoming.

I knew I already had cancer in my bones; let's just toss in some from the inner rib muscle next to my lung.

At end of the day my sister posts that people should not expect any personal updated from me, not tonight and probably not even tomorrow.

"The most important thing she can do for herself now is get as much rest as possible," she posts. "She's on some pretty strong pain meds and hopefully today's surgery will help alleviate some of the back pain and chest pain she was having."

Chapter 12

Discharge Delays

I do not do any online status updates today. Today is a day for more tests and imaging and for recovery from surgery. These tests are unexpected, but turn out to be revealing. Radiology brings a portable x-ray machine into my room and takes several images. They find a chest tube! The air space disease that surrounds the chest tube has worsened from only 24 hours ago. These changes could merely be effects secondary to the procedure. The x-rays do not detect a pneumothorax. They do, however, detect my heart. It is of normal size and shape. Breathing treatments are prescribed and begun.

I am becoming more alert. One of my daughters posts, "Mom asked me to come on here and update you all so everybody can see it. Mom's surgery went as planned yesterday and she was moved into the ICU after, which is routine for patients like her. Today she is more alert and is on a liquid diet."

Another day, another chest x-ray. I want my back to stop hurting and I want to go home. People get sick and die in hospitals. I don't want to stay here any longer than I must. The chest x-rays result in the suggestion of a loculated effusion at the right apex. Simply put, the fluid is returning to the area from which it was drained. Yesterday I was excited that I could prove I had a heart. Today they can prove my heart is slightly enlarged. One day and I go from a normal heart to an enlarged heart. I don't know if this is a temporary condition or if it will continue to get worse. I don't know what type of strain that would put on my body.

A pain management doctor visits me today. I have been restless and unable to get comfortable because of pain. We discuss the medications

I have taken before and those I am currently taking. He agrees to continue the Percocet every 4 hours, as needed. He also writes orders for OxyContin every 12 hours. I tried to explain that I can't do the OxyContin. The side effects are too real and unacceptable. He listens to me and seems to understand my concerns. He explains that he will write the order for these medications. I can decide on my own if and when I am in enough pain to take them, if I ever am. I was expected to follow up in his office after discharge for pain management and management of medications.

Today was also my first interaction with my hospital assigned oncologist, Dr. LEA. I was still unable to participate in my consult due to pain. Dr. LEA noted that I looked miserable as I was lying in bed. He noted that he would review all the records and any prior records he would be able to acquire and return to discuss treatment options and plans. He believed we could treat my condition and I that would have a good quality of life. I was not salvage; I was normal and would feel healthy again.

"Hi All! It's me again. Mom was supposed to go home today. Sadly, that isn't the case; she is really ill and will be staying roughly another week in the hospital. We will get more answers by this evening after Jay speaks with the doctors. As usual, any and all prayers would help."

I know that I have been here for several days and my health is of significant concern. I still have to have kyphoplasty surgery to repair the L1 disk in my back. It will be scheduled as soon as they can get the infection under control. Doctors are in and out, but I don't remember everything. I have a pic line placed because my veins have collapsed. I've had an abdominal CT with and without contrast performed that found the effusion still present and some collapse of the right lower lobe of my lung. It was also determined that I was having the usual side effects from the pain medications. I was getting "backed up."

The support still continues. I have so many people praying for me so that I can have the strength, courage and faith to be a warrior. I have Jay. He will make sure I have the medical care I need. He has not left my side.

The days seem to float by with disregard to any calendars or appointments. More tests, this time a MRI of my lumbar spine without contrast, an evaluation for spinal stenosis. The findings result in a compression fracture at the L1 level with evidence of marrow edema. There are significant abnormal STIR signal within the L2 vertebral body with the left abnormality being greater than the right. Additional marrow signal increases are seen in L4 and L5. These may be consistent with a metastatic disease while the fracture at L1 could be a pathologic fracture. Simply put the cancer is in my spine and the cancer broke my L1 vertebra. The bone marrow edema is how the bones react to injury or infection, they swell, and this also causes additional pain and discomfort.

Dr. EKC came in to consult for Leukocytosis. Leukocytosis, which is a fancy word for a very high white blood cell count. When they thought this infection might be atypical pneumonia I was treated with Zithromax. I have elevated influenza titers and have been on cefepime, which has shown to be effective. With the addition of Tamiflu, my lab work should be within normal ranges in the next 5 days. I have to stay in the hospital for the duration of the treatment. What began as a two, or maybe three day visit has turned into more than a week long stay. Did I say that I do not like hospitals? I now like them even less.

I meet with Dr. PH. He has reviewed the MRI from yesterday. My ability to walk has been reduced to using a walker when I am able to get out of bed. Dr. PH conducts a series of motor tests to determine if any neurological issues exist related to damage in the spinal cord. We discuss a procedure called a kyphoplasty, during which they will anesthetize me and surgically implant a cement type material into my vertebrae to relieve the pain and repair the fracture. He would also like another MRI this time of the thoracic and cervical spine areas. Radiation to the spine should be considered by my radiation oncologist after I am discharged from the hospital. My final MRI is scheduled on the nineteenth of September.

I agree to the procedure. Not much time passes after both doctors are finished with their consults than it is time for another chest x-ray. There have been no changes in my lungs, and my heart has returned back to its normal size.

The results of my MRI are consistent with cancer in my bones, left side rib fracture and a malignant pleural effusion with associated atelectasis. More tests that confirm what I thought I already knew. I have cancer in my bones and the cancer that is in my inner chest wall will continue to aggravate my lung which will continue to build up fluid. I will continue to have multilevel degenerative disease in my bones because of the cancer cells.

Chapter 13

The Visitor

The doctor arrives during the night dressed in a black lab coat. He appeared in my room to share a message about my medical condition. Why does Jay not wake up? He states that they are going to wrap me up and send me home to die. This doctor dressed in dark clothes just told me I was to die. It was time to get everything in order so that I could do as the doctor said. After all, they do know the most intimate medical conditions a person has.

Arrangements must be discussed for my sister, my dogs, and my boyfriend. I had to leave them, but I did not need to leave them in a state of confusion and panic. It was important that the needs of each be foremost in my mind before I can die. The oldest dog, my old man, could not handle a major life change. The hardest decision of all was made in what felt like an instant. My poodle, Thor, he could not be happy without traveling to and from work with his next owner. Who would be capable of taking him daily out and about? My sister, only one person could be responsible enough for her. My younger sister always wanted a daughter. Would she be the right person for my 15 year old child? What about the joy of my life. Without me he would willingly become a hermit. The best person to get him over my death would be his mother. She would not let him shut out the world.

Too much thinking, time to sleep and prepare my mind for what was to come. I need to relax my mind as well as my body so that I can heal. I believe in the use of directed mental imagery to heal the body and to control pain and discomfort. I practice breathing slowly and focus my mind on warriors floating in the i.v. and being pushed into my body to heal me. They slash the infection with their swords and while many die in the battle a few continue to live on.

I think again about the doctor. Which of my records did he read that helped him come to the conclusion that I would die? How will death happen? Will I hurt like my mom did? I need to remember to tell everyone to wash their hands, I must be insistent on observing them wash their hands before they touch me. Unwashed hands can be carriers for infections. I do not want a systemic infection like my mother had. Her death was painful until she became unresponsive. I don't want to die like that, I really don't.

How does one die so that the event causes the least amount of grief? How does a person truly prepare and protect others? Why is death, such a mystery?

Chapter 14

Respite for Jay

Today is another social networking day. Tori messages everyone:

"Hey everyone, its Tori again. Mom asked me to come on here and let everybody know her spirits are high and she is going into surgery tomorrow for her back, but what she really wants is a manicure pedicure. She sounds perky on the phone which is good. I'm optimistic right now, I think we all can be for the mean time."

Today I ask my online support system if anyone was willing to spend Tuesday night at hospital with me, to relieve Jay and to be my advocate. Friends and family alike send their regrets, my daughter sadly posting the she's sorry she's not here to help, my sister stating she wishes that she could be here with me. One of my friends says that he's covering for his wife on Tuesday while she's at school, but that he'd love to stop in on Saturday. Another offers to spend a few hours on Tuesday, staying after 8:30 that night when she got out of work, but that she'd have to be back at work at 8:45.

I respond to everyone the best I can. I tell my friend who offered to stop by after work that YES, even a few hours respite is helpful. We arrange for my friend to call Jay tomorrow. I reassure my friend in Orlando that he's not a "crappy friend!" He needs to keep his pink wig close at hand. Jay might need another relief night.

I reassure my daughters, telling one that she is doing other work for us and the other that she and Matt are right where I need them. Telling Kris, I could not do some of what must be done if Matt lived here. Why do you think I pushed you to leave when I only had gut feelings? When you get past guilt I have job I need you to do for me.

My friend and her mother both spent several hours with me at the hospital. They went on a scavenger hunt to find the only thing I had asked for, a banana Slurpee! That drink made my night! We talked and laughed and I coughed. I shared my tattoos with them. Even my daughters and sisters had not seen them. Our party lasted less than six hours, as Jay made his way back to the hospital at two o'clock in the morning. For him to find us awake and enjoying our girl party brought the sweetest smile to his face. I can't wait to see more of those.

I have to write. There is a poem inside that must get put onto paper. I have this urgency and I don't understand.

A Journey of Beaches

For two weeks you carried me, my head, rested on your shoulder
while your arms supported my sore back and weary legs.

You walked me on that beautiful California beach.
White sand cliffs and black rock it was here my fear began to leave.

The next day you carried me, we went to white pristine beaches
no evidence of humans anywhere it was here I learned to listen to
stillness

A bit later the sand was black you laughed and the water diamonds
appeared

Dolphins and whales danced this beach showed great beauty in all
forms of life.

That final beach, was barren. The water still in pain.
Somberly, quietly, you carried me. Here, I learned how lacking I am in
compassion

My journey it was over, I am able to stand.
You are still beside me, holding my hand.

I will grow weary, I will be weak,
and I have more lessons to learn, but many more lessons to teach.

My life as my bones, are fragile and sore.
I remain here for my pleasure. I remain here to share your lessons.

I asked that you carry, each friend in need I have.
By your reassurance, you have. Each with a beach unique to them.

I will never be strong enough, to walk this journey alone.
There are people on my path, which will step in to help.

Thank you for the beaches, the lessons and the love.
Your gentle guidance touched me, bringing me that innocence…

That I've neglected to nurture.

Together

Anger and frustration, fear of loss in control.
The days were the worst, any man should enter.

Order and safety, cleanliness and health.
Things you think you can control, emphasize the lack of flight can't.

We journey together, this path destined to be mine.
Over the sunlit hills, and down through the dark valleys.

We traveled together, drawing strength as a team.
What I lack you will have, as I will have for you.

At the end of our journey, there will be an end.
We can look back at how we shared our strengths, weaknesses,
above all, our love sent our dreams.

We lived our lives fully, loved with a passion.
What was mine is yours.
The memories together, always ours.

Chapter 15

Your Room is Not Ready

Time has passed. How much? I do not know. All I know is that I am awake. Jay and I have had lots of talks. Jay crawls up into the hospital bed and gently takes me in his arms. Crying he says that he does not want me to die, he begs me to live. He tells me that he can't live without me. I tell him of the pink warriors inside my body covering the white tumors on my chest wall and how they forfeit their life to become part of me and heal the tumor lesions. I'm trying hard to get more warriors but the tumor grows faster than the pink warriors arrive. He says he wants to go inside to heal me, to think of him as my white knight charging in to kill the cancer. I can't let him in. He would die. I tell him no, but to send in his soldiers. We are both crying and exhausted from this discussion.

I just finished reading my email on my cell phone. My eye is tired. Time to close my left eye and let it rest. My right eye sees at a distance rather well, but not up close so I don't use it for reading the cellphone. I am exhausted. It must be close to time to go. I ask God for one small request. I don't mind leaving my family if he truly wants me to join him. He knows when it is right and proper. I just ask that I not have pain. Please God, don't let me hurt like my mother did. I don't want those that love me to feel guilty for touching me and causing pain. I trust him to take care of those I love.

Behind me is a voice, it hurts to try to turn. I can't see who is talking to me. When did this man come into my room? When did I fall asleep?

What do you want?

"Listen carefully to what I have to say. I have not prepared your room; I am not ready for you. This is your future, watch the movie carefully so you can be prepared."

The television disappears and a pure white screen, beautiful white, so pretty and easy to look at. Children. Children in my future. I do not usually like children. In fact, I mostly do not like children at all. Why would they be in my future? The children are gathering in front of a couch for a photo.

Again I need to see it again please.

"Of course you may."

Black-and-white film plays. Children are laughing and running around. Parents gather them in the living room for a family photo. I am part of the movie and not quite yet part. Who are the children? The young parents start showing their faces. Two of them I recognize, but I know them much younger. One is Tina, my sister and she is fifteen years old. When did she grow up so much? She looks beautiful and she has a baby of her own. I can't see the man with her, however.

The other woman I recognize is Annabelle, my oldest granddaughter. She is seven years old as I remember her, now, but in this movie she is a college age girl. Laughing and calling for her Memaw. Wait, that is me, I'm Memaw. Is this movie truly my future? I get to see my grandkids grow up! I strain to try and turn around and the room turns white. It is no longer important to say anything, I feel peaceful and calm.

"Rest child, you have much to do when you wake up."

I am awake.

I have much to do.

I have to live.

I have to trust.

I must forgive completely as I was forgiven.

I believe I defeated Satan by letting go and letting God.

Chapter 16

Get Off My Train

I'm sick and tired of the small comments and fears that people make, writing my life off! Only God knows if I have less than a year to live or more than a year to live! I am fighting to live, not living to die. Join me or get off my train. I expect people to smile and be happy. I have some pain that is controlled by mild narcotics. I must have back surgery for the fractured disk. It is a twenty minute process! Chemo? Been there, done that! Radiation? Been there, done that!

This cancer will never conquer my spirit. Learn something from that; don't learn to accept finality of life. I love and respect each and every one of you! Please, do not expect me to roll over and die. It is difficult to listen to family give you permission to die and then offer to take care of your loved ones for you. This behavior, sending me to an early grave, is unacceptable. I will live; I KNOW I CAN, I KNOW I CAN, and I will prove it to you!

Make a Plan. Live the Plan. Always have contingencies available.

My back surgery is delayed another day.

Coughing. Deep, retching cough. Pain. When will this end? I coughed so hard that I broke my collarbone. The first x-ray shows that the bone is not fractured. One side of the bone is extended away from the other side. There is a lump on my collarbone and the x rays show no fracture? I know it is not right. I have a broken bone! The images are wrong. How will I be able to have my back surgery with a broken collarbone? The technician says that sometime fractures don't appear on film for up to three days. How does that fix the pain and fracture now if they can't find proof for up to three days?

Please stop all the pain.

"It's Tori," my daughter posts, "Mom coughed and possibly fractured/broken her collarbone. Moving to X-ray, more updates later."

A team member from my three-day breast cancer walk team shared the news that, in her words, I am "AMAZING. No broken collarbone! God answered our prayers on that one today and is watching over her and the doctors caring for her. Good news is that they have come up with a plan of attack that she is excited about! I'll let her share the details but I am so very pleased that they are thinking outside of the box with our special friend."

Sadly, although I know and believe that God is looking out for me, the future images show that the collarbone is actually fractured. The x-rays that show otherwise are wrong. As a result of the inaccurate films I will always have a misaligned collarbone.

Chapter 17

Sinkhole!

I speak to the nurse about better pain management control. I'm allergic to both natural- and synthetic-based codeine. She recommends I take the Oxycontin that I have orders for.

I explain that I've taken Oxycontin before. It gives me the same hallucinations that I get when I take Tylenol 3 or any other codeine-based narcotic. She reassures me that Oxycontin will work better than morphine. I'll be able to get a good night sleep before my surgery tomorrow. If I have negative side effects they can be eliminated through the I.V. drip. I reluctantly agree to try the drug, again.

Night falls. I take my medication for pain. I am terrified of the side effects. Where will I go tonight? What will I see? I'm so glad Jay understands my fears and is willing to make sure I don't suffer hallucinations. I close my eyes.

Dear God please help me! The earth just opened up beneath my feet. I see the roots from the tree. Quickly I grasp a root and drive my toes into the soft dirt. The dark brown dirt crumbles and falls away. I can't keep my feet lodged into the soil. I can see the grass; it is just one arm reach away. Which hand do I release from the tree root so I can grab solid land? Which one, my left or my right hand? Oh, not my left hand. The pain is excruciating, Just trying to reach for the ground causes my arm to fall off. I only have one hand to hold on to the root. The other arm is gone, it just fell off, and I can't watch it fall to the ground. I just can't.

The root is white and thick and my hand is not able to completely wrap around it. As the dirt drops and exposes whiter root my hand slips. Squeeze tighter. I have to squeeze tighter. I try again to drive my feet into the soft soil under the tree.

I am still holding on, but the root is being pulled out of the soil and away from the tree. I will not let go. I can't fall, it is not an option. The root, it is in my hand, but not in the soil. It has pulled away from the ground and now I slowly spin in a 360 degree circle. I see dirt on all sides of me, but nothing that will provide me a safe landing. The gaping empty hole descends below me. No ledges or cliffs. There is just soft dirt that drops freely below. The dirt swallows up the small branches and roots that fall there. Is this what a sink hole looks like? It is only soft dark dirt without any bottom? A limb falls past me. It lands in the soft dirt below and slowly sinks down and below the surface. I watch fascinated as the brown bark disappears and the leafy top slowly gets sucked under. Only a single leaf is left. It is as if the dirt swallowed up the branch and left a single leaf as a reminder of its power. If I fall like that branch, my body will be swallowed up in the soft soil. It will compress my bones and organs. I will be crushed but still breathing. The leaf would be my head. The opportunity to be rescued and pulled out would happen. I would be a broken crushed body. Paralyzed and dependent on others to provide all my needs this is terrible. I can't think that way. But is it better than dying? No. Being totally dependent on others for basic care is worse than death. I need to stop thinking of this. It's time to pull myself up the root. It is time to move forward away from the dirt, climb higher and higher. Get safe.

The sound of cracking and creaking invade my thoughts. The tree is leaning into the hole. Maybe, no not with just one hand I can't. I want my other arm back. It's there! I have two arms again. I reach carefully for the tree. I just know I can scramble up the tree and get on the ground. I'll be safe on the ground. I have to hurry there is not any time to waste thinking how to move upward. Left hand over right hand slowly slides each hand over the other and up the white root. The tree trembles. I'm at the trunk. I can swing my leg over the trunk and then jump onto the ground. I'll be safe.

The tree collapses onto me. It drags me into the deep dark brown hole.

72

"Jay, help me!"

I scream. I'm crying and falling. Down, down, down. Will the falling ever stop? The tree falls faster and separates from my grasp. I am descending into the pit of the earth without anything to hold on to head over heels I fall. I try to grab the sides but the dirt crumbles under my fingers as I desperately try to find a secure hold. Jay. Please, help me.

Warm, soft arms grab me and pull me out of my death spiral. Jay, he caught me. I awake.

"Please keep holding me," I say.

I tell him of my dream and he reassures me I am safe. I close my eyes believing him. I start falling again. I'm ripped out of his arms and down through the ground I spiral spinning like a top faster and faster as I descend.

"Karen open your eyes, I'm here."

Again I'm safe.

We call the nurse. The terror stops.

Chapter 18

Every Spine needs a bit of Cement

Time for the kyphoplasty procedure. I'm told this procedure is a simple one. I will be given a local sedative and mild anesthesia to undergo the surgery. I will be lying face down on the table. The doctor will make two small incisions into my back and insert a small drill. He will drill through the bony portion of my L1 vertebra and will insert bone cement into the cavity. This procedure will restore the proper height of the disc and take the pressure off the nerves. Then, if all goes well, my back will stop hurting!

I'm in pre-op for the kyphoplasty procedure. I tell them about the collarbone and how much it hurts. I am given a choice: I can choose not to have my back repaired or I can be laid on my chest with my arms spread and know that the medication will not allow me to remember the pain in my collarbone. I'm anxious and upset but the only choice is to get my spine repaired. My spine is the bigger issue here, bigger than the collarbone pain. I agree to take the medicine and get my spine fixed.

The only thing I remember is rolling off the bed and onto the operating table where I stretch my arms out and slip into peaceful oblivion before waking in my room with Jay standing beside the bed, talking to me. My back pain was gone.

Maybe, tomorrow I can find out about chemo and then go home after my first treatment.

Post-operative report of Dr. PH, surgeon:

After the patient was taken to the operating room, MAC anesthesia was successfully administered. The patient was positioned in the prone

74

position. The lumbar region was prepped and draped in typical sterile fashion. Lidocaine was infiltrated into the skin. Spinal needle was passed down to the L1 pedicle. The operative level was confirmed.

The L1 pedicle was cannulated bilaterally with Jamshidi needles. A percutaneous bone biopsy was performed through the Jamshidi cannula. Course was drilled into the vertebral body through both pedicles. The balloons were inflated in the vertebral body of L1. The cement was introduced into the vertebral body. There was approximately 3 cc of cement introduced maybe 4 cc just before there was some extavasation toward the posterior pedicle wall. The infiltration of cement was terminated due to the extension of the cement posteriorly toward the posterior cortex of the L1 vertebra. There was some slight extravasation of cement into the L1-L2 disk space and then further cement infiltration was terminated in that location also. AP and lateral fluoroscopy demonstrated adequate filling of the L1 vertebral body. The cannulas were withdrawn. Incisions were closed with 4-0 Vicryl and Steri-Strips and sterile dressing was applied. The patient was taken to the recovery room in stable condition.

Chapter 19

Discharge Orders

At ten o'clock pm the doctor comes in to the room to tell me I am being discharged. My kyphoplasty was an outpatient process, so no reason exists to keep me in the hospital any longer. I have more choices. I must decide if I am to be discharged to a nursing home or to hospice. I believe that neither option is acceptable. I don't want to go home until tomorrow. It's late. I argue with the doctor that Jay and I need to sleep. The doctor insists that remaining in the hospital is not an option. We must be discharged tonight. After discussing our options, we decide that if they can get a hospice intake manager in to accept me tonight we will go that route. I am hoping that by eleven o'clock the program will be closed and we will have to wait for morning. Despite these hopes, the intake case manager shows up to get the medical forms completed so that I can go home tonight.

I am extremely unhappy about the decision to send me home tonight. Over the course of the stay at the hospital, I have been given a myriad of final diagnoses. I have a large pleural effusion secondary to metastatic breast cancer status post thoracostomy and pleurodesis with pleural biopsy. Stage IV breast cancer with metastasis to the pleural space and bones. L1 compression fracture status post kyphoplasty. Major depression. Secondary hypoparathyroidism. Rib fractures. Electrolye imbalance including hypokalemia. Post-op ileus. Hypercalcemia. Hypomagnesaemia. Hypothyroidism. The list seems endless and beyond comprehension. My condition is stable but guarded. I'll be following up with the oncologist and for radiation treatments after discharge.

Why do doctors automatically assume that if you have a diagnosis of cancer you must be depressed? I'm not suffering from major depression. I am dealing with major pain and it is not an automatic connection that one must be accompanied by the other.

Before I leave the hospital I'll be given an injection of Lupron. Jay begins to load up the car to take me home. We are asked if anyone from hospice brought the oxygen in for me to use on the way home. If I don't have oxygen I'll have to wait to be transported home by ambulance and that can take several hours to arrange. At this point, we just want to go home and get some sleep.

A nurse arrives in the room while Jay is out. She tells me she has my injection. I ask what size needle and how thick it is. I want to know if the injection will hurt more than a tetanus shot. She informs me that it will be much more painful than a tetanus shot. I begin to cry. I beg her to wait until Jay returns from downstairs. I send him a text, asking him to hurry back and tell him why. The nurse refuses to wait, she lifts the edge of my gown and tells me to show the hip. I lay there crying while she injected the Lupron.

The injection is not as painful as she described. Why would she want to scare me that way? I am still crying when Jay returns. He gathers me into his arms and holds me until I calm down. This discharge is rapidly becoming a nightmare. I refuse to let anyone know how terrorized I feel. I post online that I am headed home and everyone responds enthusiastically.

Tonight's discharge feels like a mistake. The discharge nurse tells me if I have any complications I can return to the emergency room tomorrow. I can only hope that the doctor is not making a mistake and that I will not be coming back tomorrow. Her words cannot be prophetic!

Hospice delivers the oxygen, bed, wheelchair, walker all to my home while we are processing through discharge. It is hard to believe the doctors are saying I only have three months to live. I cannot fathom that, it is impossible.

Chapter 20

Do Not Resuscitate

I have arrived home from the hospital. Inside, the hospice nurse is waiting for me along with the intake worker. Hospice means death, dying, forever being just a memory. As I walk slowly through the door, I see there's now a hospital bed in the dining room. The sheets on it are pink. The pillow has my favorite shell pillowcase on it, ready to be used. I may never sleep in my own bed again. Two individuals from Hospice are there, seated at our long dining room table. I lower my aching body into the brown leather chair and Jay slides the chair close to the table. It's time to sign the paperwork for the final stage of my life.

Much of that morning remains a blur, the speed at which papers are slid across the table for me to sign. I can't process the information, the experience, so fast. Why such a rush? The Hospice nurse slides an orange piece of paper in front of me.

"You now need to sign this form," she says.

I ask her what form is.

"It's a DNR," she says.

A DNR is a "do not resuscitate" form. I'm not ready to sign this form. I'm not ready to admit I am going to die. I don't care what the doctor says. I don't care what Hospice says. I will not sign this form!

The nurse emphatically describes the process involved with resuscitation. She explains that I need to understand that if, for any reason, I lose consciousness and stop breathing or if my heart stops, the paramedics are legally obligated to restart my breathing and my heartbeat. They're going to apply chest compressions. These compressions are going to be applied with such force that they will crush my ribs. The fragments of my crushed ribs will penetrate into my lungs. My lungs will collapse; I will need to be intubated. Instead of dying a natural peaceful death I will be hooked up to machines and Jay will have to fight to allow me to die. I remember when my mother signed her DNR worksheet. It was not the kindest thing she could do for us. It was a clinical, cold process. It was not handled in a "kind" manner.

I tell Jay that I am not ready to give up. I am not ready to die. I am not willing to sign the DNR form.

"You must sign the form," the nurse insists. "It's the nicest thing you can do for your family."

I start crying and look at Jay. "I'm not ready please," I say.

Jay looks at the nurse. "Karen is not signing the form," he tells her.

What's next?

"The form will be signed," the hospice nurse says, "but I agree it won't be tonight."

She's displeased. I don't care. What gives her the right to decide whether it is all right or not for me to sign the form? It is my decision. I have a problem with people in authority pushing that authority beyond my limits. I take control of the conversation.

"Who will be on my medical team?" I ask her. "What color team will I be assigned to?"

I learn that I am have been assigned to the same color as my mother was when she became a hospice patient. My social worker is the young lady who is seated at the table with us. She is the same young lady who guided us through my mother's death last year. The nurse seated with us says she is the registered nurse who will be managing my care.

"Who is my medical doctor? What's the procedure for seeing him or her?"

"The doctor only meets with hospice patients one time," the hospice nurse explains. "I will handle all of the communications with him concerning your care and your health. If you need additional visits to any medical appointments you just call me and I'll have them authorized."

The nurse then proceeds to explain the process by which her weekly visits will follow. I've got her number, she says. Next week, when she comes to visit me, I know how to make her visits less stressful on me. I will focus the discussions on what she is doing and how her days are going. This method of coping will be acceptable for now. I am yawning I need to go to sleep. The intake process is wrapped up and Hospice departs for the night.

Hospice is an insurance company that provides services to allow me to live as fully and as completely on my terms as I can while I die. I must learn how to manage their various medical personnel. It will take me a few weeks to learn how to navigate the many medical appointments, as well. I want to go to school. I intend to do whatever it takes to make that happen.

A 50-foot-long clear oxygen tube is snaked across the floor. It reaches from just outside our bedroom door to the table at which I am sitting. It's time to walk to our room and go to sleep. This walk will be another long walk. Each step I take is energy draining. I make it as far the bed hospice brought with them to the house. The mattress is firm. An inflated pad has been placed on top of it. I gather my energy and my breath sitting on the edge of the bed. Just sitting there brings tears to my eyes. I have just returned from spending many nights and days in one of these beds. The discomfort and pain from that bed has not yet left my muscles or bones. I want to sleep in my own bed.

I take the tubing in my hand and begin to walk slowly toward the bedroom. I can make it. Okay, maybe not. In my head, it's an easy stroll. In reality, I can only make it two more steps. Jay brings a rolling dining room chair to push me to our bedroom. I can't walk the length of the dining room without becoming completely exhausted, but I am happy to be home and am more than ready to go to bed.

I stand by the side of the bed, staring at it. I can't climb up into it. I won't be able to sleep in it. Frustration finally takes hold. So this is life now, compromise because of inability. I turn to Jay and ask him to take me back out to the other room, I'll sleep on the hospice bed. Jay refuses to let me do so. He guides me to the recliner near the sliding glass door and asks me to wait there. My daughter, Stefanie and Jay then proceed to partially disassemble our bed and place the bedspring directly onto the floor and then reassemble the mattress and bedding. I can sleep in our own bed. It feels like the first of many miracles. Jay gently helps me into bed and tucks me in. I swiftly drift off to sleep when I feel his arms surround me.

Chapter 21

A Spoonful of Energy

Last night was a long night. I still have no endurance or energy this morning, but I need to get up. Jay helps me swing my legs over the edge of the bed. With his arm around my waist, he almost carries me to the bathroom. He helps me dress, a task that seems to go on forever. We reverse the process from last night, using a dining room chair to wheel me out to the living room. Jay sets up my laptop for me.

"Stay put until I get back," he says.

My friends and family start posting on my page to welcome me home before I even wake up. I receive a good reminder about my limitations from one of my friends, putting my frustration from last night into perspective. "Good morning sweet girl," she posts, "Hope you are feeling much better today. Remember we must crawl before we walk, so take baby steps and do not try to overdo." I need to remember to take my baby steps and not overdo. I also have to remind myself not to get frustrated with myself when I try to overdo.

I decide to implement the spoonful of energy program. Every activity requires a spoonful of energy and I must make sure I have 2 spoons left at the end of the day. I plan my first day on 6 spoons of energy. I wake up and get dressed, first spoon used. Breakfast, Lunch, 2 more are now gone and the day is only half finished. I have one spoon left to account for any activity I want to do until dinnertime. All too soon, I use that up without thinking about it.

I can see the lake and the birds from where I sit. Outside the sliding glass door is a large screened in patio with a recliner just waiting for me to lie on. I can soak up the healing rays of the sun without getting overheated. The large lake is just at the edge of the yard. The whisper of the small waves as they flow towards the yard reminds me of how water heals the body. In flows the water and when it flows out it takes the cancer and pain and fear. I will recover because of who I am, who is with me and where I am.

Just a few steps away, Jay is making my breakfast. I don't know if I can eat or how much. I need to try, since I've lost so much weight already. Stefanie is here so Jay can go into the office for a few hours. He has been away from work for over two weeks now. He needs to go back to work on Monday. I have him home for three more days.

Caregiver responsibilities are enormous. I need assistance in everything I do. We must keep the strain from being too much on him. I believe—no, I know—I can accomplish miracles in three days and help relieve that stress. Realistically I can set small goals. My first goal is to be able to use my "Blue Dog" walker to help me get to the bathroom while he is at work. My walker has two small wheels on the base and two non-skid plates at the rear. The metal is a beautiful metallic bright blue. I have a blue basket attached with bungee cords to the front of the walker. The basket has a red and white no smoking sign attached. Blue Dog is going to help me reclaim my life.

Walking from the recliner in the bedroom to the bathroom is a task that I can certainly accomplish. I rally the energy to use Blue Dog during the day, single steps at first and then more each time as the day goes on. I get to where I can walk to the bathroom all by myself. That short walk is a major step in the right direction. If I can walk, I can manage to do other things. I can dress myself. I can keep my own house and go places on my own. I can and I will go back to college. I'm not going to die. Every day just one step more than the day before and that will give me the strength needed to live another day.

I believe that my friends will want to visit and I ask only that they take necessary health precautions such as washing their hands, I also ask that they avoid coming over if they believe they might be getting sick. I'm excited and can't wait to have friends sit at the table and share their time with me. I know someone will call and want to come see me today. I feel it in my bones. It is a quiet day at home, just the four of us, until Jay gets home. Maybe, tomorrow someone will want to come and visit.

The day ends with my daughter making our dinner and Jay helping her. After dinner, Jay and I talk about how much help Stefanie was while I was in the hospital. She came down by Greyhound bus and spent almost a week here taking care of Tina and the dogs. I knew she was here, I did not realize how much she had done or how much help she was. I wish she could stay a few more days, but now that I'm home she needs to get back home to her family.

I received a package in the mail today. I used Blue Dog to walk to the door and gather what was left by UPS. Inside the box I find that Neemah has arrived. Neemah is a Rock Star bear, a gift from my daughter and grandchildren. They went to the Build-A-Bear store and created him. Their voices are recorded in Neemah's paw pads. Can you imagine that a stuffed bear would bring such great joy? Those recordings bring them "right here."

I use social media to tell them that Neemah has arrived and that she is a Rock Star and will help me fight like a girl!

I seem to need lots of sleep and I get a few precious visitors. Social media continues to be a huge part of my recovery. Being online is a way to continue to have contact with the world outside the family room. They range from positive instances of survivors on Hospice Care to offers of food and company. One of my friends offers a comforting story about another stage 4 breast cancer patient who was given less than 6 months to live. After two years she was finally removed from hospice and lived much longer than they ever thought possible. Such miracles do happen. Can they happen to me?

I'm scheduled to begin my appointments with my radiation doctor. If I am healthy enough to make these appointments there has to be a way that I can go back to class. I need to do more than just sit in a chair and play on the laptop and sleep. It is impossible to walk without using my Blue Dog walker but I have to keep taking just one more step. I want to be in class. I want to be a productive member of society for as long as I am alive. I need a purpose and right now, school is that purpose. I have completed my simulation so that they can "map" the areas of my body that will receive radiation treatments. It can take up to two weeks to have a plan and begin treatment. I hope by then I can have a plan in place so I can be back in class.

Chapter 22

Trials and Tribulations

Who am I trying to fool? Me? Or my friends? I guess just me. Cancer hurts all the time. Cancer hurts so much it drains me. I left for the hospital just over a month ago. I was walking independently. I was able to carry my school books and shower and dress. Now I have to wake up Jay in the middle of the night to be taken to the bathroom. I can't get out of bed by myself. I can't shower by myself. I can't stand in the kitchen long enough to make a simple bowl of cereal for breakfast. I can't do it. I am trying to take care of myself. I have to keep remembering to take it slower than I am used to doing.

This month has been a trial. I wake up in the morning and wait for help to get out of bed. Then I'm pushed to the bathroom in the wheelchair, where I'm transferred onto the commode. Yes, there are unspoken steps included there. Exhausted from just this much effort I'm back in the wheelchair to rest for a few moments while Jay brushes my hair. After that brief rest, I am then able to stand up and brush my teeth. Back into the wheelchair. All this time Jay stays by my side to provide support and balance. Next, it is time to be dressed. Still more work for Jay. Breakfast to eat and gah! I don't want to eat. It is work.

It *is* work. Then I think of what Jay has already accomplished this morning. Two loads of laundry have been washed, dried, and put away. The routine of sending our teenager off to school has completed. It is only the beginning.

Soon, Jay will drive to work. At lunchtime, he will drive the thirty minutes home to make sure I eat and get any other assistance I need. He will make lunch for the both of us to share, serve lunch, and encourage me to eat one more bite each time I think I've finished. He is exhausted, but must make the thirty-minute drive back to work and finish his day there. I spend the afternoon in the recliner watching television, sleeping or playing on the computer while he is back at work managing construction issues and resolving conflicts.

By six o'clock, Jay is home and again continues to go nonstop. He undertakes more household responsibilities that were not his before. Shopping for dinner on his way home, making the meal so that I get the protein I should have, along with the fruits and vegetables. Again, he encourages me to eat "one more bite." After dinner we visit for a few minutes until he is ready to clean the kitchen while I sit and watch.

All too soon it is time for me to go to the recliner again. This time I use the walker to make the journey with my oxygen tube hanging beside me. Jay takes slow steps with me and lifts the front of the walker onto the carpet so that I can get into the bedroom. I don't have the strength at the end of the day to do more than slide my feet, but Jay has to find the strength and energy to do even more. His day doesn't stop just because he tucks me in to rest.

By ten o'clock, Jay has accomplished all the tasks at home. Our teenager is finished with her homework and in her room for the night. Exhausted, he falls asleep in his recliner next to mine. Grateful to have him close, I close my eyes for a time. Later, we will go to bed. But for now, resting here is wonderful.

Chapter 23

Taking Away The Pain

Today we start the plan to return my body to one of no pain and living as I mean to do. Jay has taken the morning off to drive me to another appointment with my radiation doctor. We park in the blue space assigned for those with handicaps. I'll take it. He walks around the car and unloads the Blue Dog and Thor to bring to my door. I hand him my portable oxygen tank and insist that I can walk to the door. I make it! I am out of breath and we have to turn up the oxygen, but I make it from the car to the lobby of the office. I'm exhausted and having a hard time breathing and collapse onto the padded chair, but I am so proud of myself, deep down I'm jumping for joy.

Dr. K., Jay and I determine together a plan to start treating the most painful areas first. Pain equals cancer growth and bone destruction. Radiation will destroy the cancer cells in the bones and allow those areas to heal and eliminate the pain. I ask if I will hurt when this is done and I'm assured that the purpose of this type of treatment is to reduce or eliminate the pain. Less pain is better than constant pain.

Today we began radiation on my left hip. Sometimes I wish I could just say "they" began the radiation and stay out of the picture! The treatments will continue for eleven weekdays. Coordinating transportation to and from these appointments will be a challenge. I don't know how long Jay can take time off of work to keep being my primary driver and caregiver. I can't wait until I can drive again. I know that I am going to have to learn to ask for help. Maybe.

Radiation treatment is simply a matter of lying on a metal table and being still. The machine does all the work. Even so, I tense up the minute the machine begins to move around my body. I clench my fists as I fight to stay still. The machine buzzes. My hips twitch in response to the sound. I gradually relax. Three zones are radiated so that my hip will receive the maximum benefit. The machine stops buzzing. It begins to move again. The radiation beam is directed into my body to kill the cancer.

These treatments will be the "job" I go to before going to my class at Hillsborough Community College. It will continue 5 days a week until all the areas are addressed.

The nurses bring Jay into the room after the treatment is completed. He helps me get up and put my oxygen back on. Time to head to school again. This is going to be a great day!

Jay drives me to school. We pull into the employee parking area. He parks in a loading zone, which puts me as close as possible to my classroom. I have arrived a half an hour early for class, but I believe it will take every bit of that to get to my classroom and settled into a seat.

Jay brings Thor out of the car, along with Blue Dog. My algebra book, my notebook, and my portable oxygen tank are inside the basket. I am using a shorter oxygen tube today, so I can't be more than six feet away from my tank. I step between the handles of Blue Dog and wait patiently while Jay dresses Thor for the morning. Thor is wearing a green backpack that has my wallet, pens, pencils and my medications. He is positioned to my left and Jay supports me on my right. We step up the curb together and then I turn and kiss Jay goodbye. I'll see him in two hours when he arrives to take me home. I'm very excited to be able to return to class.

One step and smile, I must smile. I believe that if my fellow students see me smiling, then they have to smile back, I won't give them a choice not to. Remember, step breathe smile, step breathe smile. I can walk and breathe or talk and breathe but I can't walk, talk, and breathe at the same time. It takes ten minutes to walk the length of the college building but I make it. No, we make it. Thor has never before had to walk this slowly beside me in public. We are a team on this campus. Together we will finish the semester!

The professor watches me enter the room. Class has not yet started but students are in their seats. I take a chair on the far left of the room at the end of a row of tables. This seat allows Thor a place to lie beside me. Blue Dog is out of the way and I am protected from being bumped. As I begin to lower myself into the plastic chair my professor motions for me to wait. He brings over a padded chair with wheels. This chair will make sitting for two hours less of a strain on my spine. By the time I settle into my chair with my books on the table it is time for class to begin.

I can do this!

After class is over, my professor comes over and we have a short discussion. I explain that my breast cancer has returned and spread to my bones and the area by my lung.

"My wife had breast cancer, too," he says. "May I make a suggestion? You should probably consider dropping this class. Focus on getting your treatments and getting healthy."

He doesn't know the reason for my being in school, I don't feel comfortable telling him that without the ability to attend class I feel less of a human, less worthy. I want to be productive and get healthy and I need to be in school to do that. I compromise with myself and explain to him that I can't stop class. I need to be here for me and, if I drop the class I lose the money spent for the class. I'd like to stay in class, even if you have to give me an incomplete for the semester.

"You know that you've missed a lot. Earning an A will be almost impossible."

"I understand. I can handle that." Class will be two days a week. I know I will have enough time at home to catch up on past assignments. I can do this.

The walk back to the parking lot is again the smile-step routine. I like this routine. It's amazing the effect of a smile on the expressions of others. Jay tucks me into the car and latches the seat belt, puts Thor and Blue Dog in the car, and takes us all home. I'm exhausted. It has been a very long morning and I plan to take a nap when I get home.

Chapter 24

Asking for Help

Every breath I take is one more breath for which I am thankful. It is by a miracle I am here to take it. Regarding the teenager, she still hides in her room and huffs me on everything. It is easier to not ask and slowly do myself. Learning not to ask for help that is the lesson she is teaching me. She just does not know it.

Yes, it's a down day. Not so much because I have to ask total strangers for help, but because I have to ask people I have never met to help since those I have met are not able to be here to help. It isn't so much the teenager who is having a hard time adjusting to my new normal that is the problem. Rather, it is the person who committed to helping me anytime I need it who, when I call, tells me that I have asked too late for them to help and I should have asked a few days prior. I'm amazed that anyone would think I could control the schedules of others and not need last minute help. I feel as if I was such an inconvenience to everyone. And yet, the consensus is that it's fine for me to ask for help, it's even important for me to do so. "Why are you depriving your friends of the joy and fulfillment they will receive helping you," one asks. "Think of how good you feel when you are able to help someone out!"

I need to remember this fact. It is hard to do sometimes, when I am impatient to achieve what I want for my new normal.

Asking for help is normal, having the request rejected is not normal. I learn to make notes on who offers to help in which way and if they actually follow through willingly, and without making me feel as if I am a burden to them or inconvenience in their daily schedules. It really is easier to not ask for any help and just accept that less is the new normal. This can be considered as new goals for me to meet. New objectives to strive for. A new normal in the future, one different from this current state of normal. I look back at how far I have already progressed. I am back in school and able to walk with a walker. I am getting stronger and more independent.

Chapter 25

I Will Always Stand Back Up

Warning for cancer! I will stand back up! You'll know the moment when I have just had enough! Sometimes I'm afraid, and don't feel that tough, but I will stand back up! Your time in this body is over! I am a cancer assassin and I will destroy you with all the tools and resources available to me! I am victorious! Praise god!

My sister challenges my cancer. She posts, "dear cancer: you picked the wrong girl to pick on; she has an army of friends and family backing her up! You better stand down cancer so my sister can stand up! Fight like a girl sis! I love your attitude; it means you're feeling a little better. 3 months and I will visit you!"

Jay has fallen asleep in the recliner. I'm not quite ready or able to get up and into bed on my own yet, so I wait until he wakes up to go to bed.

It is important that I practice being strong until being strong is no longer just practice. Gaining interior strength is the same as gaining physical strength, it takes patience and it takes training. I need to work

I have a program for the computer called Skype. I'm just learning how to use it and need to get a microphone still. It opens up new possibilities for visiting and arranging my schedule. I still have people asking to see me and I still need to get back and forth at times when Jay is not available. I'm fortunate in that sometimes people are willing to combine the two.

Not much sleep again last night. My spine just does not want to cooperate with allowing sleep, and when I do get to where I can sleep, the collarbone then complains. Darned if I do or don't. It is bone pain.

The doctors said muscle soothers won't work. Just a few more days, they reassure me, and radiation treatments will take most of the pain away. All I know is that something must change. I stay awake and pray for friends, sleep, and elimination of pain. I remember it could be worse so I enjoy the silence of the night and revel in living.

Even so, I need sleep to be able to function. Last night, I stayed up until I was too tired to stay awake, I kept busy on my computer, but still I couldn't sleep well. I consider the idea of a stiff drink tonight, maybe. An ice pack, too. Neither will cure the problem, but both will help relieve the pain.

Tonight Tina and Jay have gone out to see Carrie Underwood in concert. A new friend gave us a pair of tickets they were unable to use at the last minute. I am so glad that Jay and Tina are going. I know they will enjoy it. When I get healthy enough for an adventure like this I'd like to go see Garth Brooks, Tim McGraw, Kiss or even Boston. My music tastes are all over the chart.

I get a text message from Jay, seems that even those that like Carrie Underwood also like to get drunk and smoke in a no smoking building. Oh, it's not cigarettes that this guy is smoking. I'm glad that the bad behavior is good for reinforcing good behavior.

I decide that crowds might not ever be an environment I want to be exposed to. I believe that I'll start looking into a hot air balloon ride or even a flight on a glider. I can envision the peace and quiet in both while floating through the air with the birds.

Tomorrow must be a significant catch up day for my math class. Both the online homework and bookwork have gotten behind. Thank goodness for books that have directions. I need to be ready for the math test on Wednesday. I'm going to head to bed early and let my night owls take care of themselves when they get home. I am looking forward to hearing about their adventure in the morning.

Chapter 26

Susan Komen 3 Day Walk

I'm still making it to Algebra class three days a week with my trusty Blue Dog walker, Thor and I. I did not pass the mid-term, but I'll not give up. I am beginning to be able to get around in the house without my walker and am looking forward to being able to get around in public without it also. I am impatient with my slow progress.

Radiation treatments are still 5 days a week. Jay has to drive me to most of them, but some friends and a few strangers have stepped up to help with transportation. It does make it a bit better for Jay when others help us this way.

The big breast cancer walk is going to be this month. The Komen event is very popular in Tampa Bay. Everyone is doing their last minute fundraising to be able to spend 3 days walking in Saint Petersburg and Clearwater.

I start planning on how I can cheer on the walkers this year. St. John's Pass was always a favorite part of the walk when Thor and I were walkers. The access to the shade was fantastic, the crowds however are not fantastic. I ask those that are planning on being at the pass if there is a better spot than other areas and find out that not only is the walk going through, but there is an annual seafood festival that weekend. This additional activity will negate the option of cheering from St. Johns Pass.

The walkers that know Thor and I start sharing that they are excited we might be able to attend as "walker stalkers". During the walk there are planned stops for food, drinks, rest and bathrooms. One of my friends is the pit stop captain for pit 5. She pops a private message and suggests that we consider hanging out for the day at her pit stop. We can set up a tent and chairs and watch as everyone walks into the pit. I'm told that just being there will inspire others to do just a "bit more" than they think they can do. Jay and I decide to set up under the shade trees at pit 5 and visit with all those walkers that know Thor and me. I am excited about the chance to be out for the day doing something different. Just a few more weeks to go the anticipation is priceless.

The Thursday prior to the event I need to coordinate a ride home from school. One of my favorite walkers is going to be on his way through town and we have made arrangements for him to pick me up after class. I will have a smile and a positive attitude about life. I will be a person, a face, a reason for him to keep fundraising and keep working towards his goals to help this organization fund research that might be able to find a cure to save my life. Thor immediately recognizes my friend and gives him the standard woo woo greeting that he has always given 3-day walkers as we walk to the parking lot. When we get home and settled in, Thor manages to climb up in Dylan's lap and pretend he is a toy poodle. My standard poodle service dog is cuddled up in the lap of a 6 foot tall guy wearing a pink wig. This was a moment for the memory books!

The walk finally begins and I am doing internet stalking and television watching. Our local news channel has two newscasters walking and it feels like there is live feed from the 3-Day. I'm catching up on my algebra and looking forward to tomorrow.

I had a blast, Saturday, hanging out under my blue tent at Pit 5. I saw many of the friends that I have walked a mile or more with in past walks. I was included in the event without having to push myself to do the event. Several walkers took time out to sit under the tent with us and shared some of the interesting things that happened while they were walking. One lady said that she had been struggling to make it to pit 5 but knew that if she swept she would be taken straight to camp and didn't want to miss us. She reminded me of perseverance. You do more just so you can have another experience. Similar to taking treatments for cancer, you have to push yourself some days just to do the minimum expected but if you don't push yourself to treat yourself right, show up for your treatments and communicate with friends you won't make it through the fight of your life.

We finally arrive home and I am exhausted. I go online and tell everyone thanks. Thank you for letting me cheer you on today. Thank you for taking the time to stop and visit with us. Thank you for your smiles. Thank you most of all for every step, every sweep, every dollar. One day more lives will be saved because of what you do this weekend.

I think back to my first 3-day walk. I walked so many miles alone. Just Thor and I. Like a journey with cancer, alone and isolated, was many miles of the walk reminded me of how cancer makes you feel. I was able to meet up with another "forgotten" walker, Anna, and we finished off that walk together. We resolved that for all future walks we would never leave another behind. Since then I have encouraged others to not leave others behind. Dylan shared that he took that advice and walked with some solo walkers, survivors and how much it impacted his day and he hoped it made their journey that much better. Because' of the journey that Anna and I took together that year, even when we walk separate events, we never walk alone.

Chapter 27

Still Smiling, Still Fighting

November has arrived and I'm still smiling and fighting this cancer. Yesterday was a good day for me. I'm still having conversations with people I met at the three-day walk. One of my new friends tells me how meeting me was a perfect way to kick off the walk weekend, how she took my advice to walk with some solo walkers and some cancer survivors. She has no idea how happy she made me when she said it "made her day" to do it and that she hoped her presence there helped make their walk better for them. It's so tremendous to hear from the people she called my "amazing backing of cheerleaders and friends who want to help me get through my cancer fight."

For the last two days I have been "walker-free." I need to get Thor groomed so he can go to work on Monday and help when I go to school. I have a great friend that has volunteered to give both dogs a bath and she shows up when she says she will! Thor is going to be a handsome dog for school Monday. I'm still using the portable oxygen when I walk and need to make sure that I pace myself appropriately.

I talk online about the "new normal" I will have at school. As excited as I am for the changes I see where others are worried I am pushing myself to hard and too fast. They want me healthy for a long time, not just here long enough.

Chapter 28

Requests and Tests

My right lung is not good today. I need prayers or will need medical intervention. Either the doctor or her nurse will evaluate my lung capacity via sound, something that is already checked on a weekly basis. Dr. K. orders a chest x-ray, MRI and sends me to see my pulmonology specialist.

The chest x-ray will help me and my medical team decide what is next. I don't worry too much. I would just like to take a deep breath. Otherwise it is just another day in the life of cancer. No big deal. So I have cancer, I have other pains also, sometimes those pains hurt more than anything else, other times the cancer hurts. But I do pretty good keeping each in their own compartment.

I share online that I will be going to be asking for help with transportation again. I ask those that can to post if they have time, energy, to drive between Brandon and Ruskin with me in the mornings. Soon I hope they will let me drive again! I never realized how "stuck" you feel when you do not drive.

At the follow up appointment after the tests are complete I'm told that the fluid is reduced from after the hospital stay in September. I have a slight chest infection which is treated with a Z-pack and that I have a new met on my number eight rib. I'm learning to adjust to different levels of pain tolerances. The radiation treatments to my spine have been killing the tumors that are pressing on the nerves. There are two additional mets on my torso that we will radiate after Christmas. My body is due for a radiation break so that it can recover from the high level of radiation that has been aimed into it for the last three months. Dr. K. says that maybe after Christmas I can start to drive again, right now she wants to get the spine issues addressed and resolved.

I am glad that the swelling I was so worried about is only another bone mets. I can live with bone mets.

Chapter 29

The Christmas Party

I want to talk, to express not only how I feel but what I am feeling. It just hurts to talk, to be willing to really open up. In addition to the stupid side effects from the cancer and treatments, I'm learning that some people are afraid to be near me because they might cause me to be sick. I have cancer, I do not currently have a depressed immune system. My blood is monitored and I'm not at risk for getting any sicker than anyone else. I'm just feeling lousy with the limited energy, sore throat, and sleepy. I can't wait until next stage of radiation is complete and that my back stops hurting. I should crawl in bed and sleep.

I feel resentful, but then my friends and family continue to post good wishes and appear to be understanding of my feelings. I am told to do it "my way," my friends and family are "more patient than I thought". These things mean so very much to me. Several seem to know that I am angry at circumstances, even if I am not angry for specific things or at specific people. One person I knew only from online games told me that she lost her father to cancer and some of her friends as well. She passed along some brilliant, if painful, words of wisdom:

Girl, be pissed off. Or make peace with it. You do what you have to do. Everyone around you is afraid for you. Your family may want to deny it. But, you are sick and it isn't going to be fun at all. I am so sorry that you have to go through this. All I can say is you do what you want and be who you are.

She reminds me that, even when I'm angry, the people who love me will be there for me and will help me through this. I know what she says is true. It's a repeated refrain, especially from people who know me only through their monitors. Another friend that I know only online reminds me that the people who are afraid to be around me for fear of making me sick are not only scared for me, because they fear making me sicker. They are afraid for themselves because they cannot or will not accept these changes, my new normal. They may or may not come around to acceptance or comprehension. This is where I learn that some will distance themselves to protect their emotional involvement, and that it has nothing to do with who I am or what I am living with.

What is important for me to do now is to take care of myself, listen to my body, and do what is best for me. She reminds me that it's all right for me to have bad days, like I am having now, or even to be scared. I know she is right. Being afraid or having a bad day is normal with cancer. It's just difficult to do when I'm being told that my positive attitude is an inspiration. My sister sends me a poignant message. I have to wonder how much her feelings are reflected in other people to whom I am close:

I don't need space to adjust; I just need to know what I can do for you. Want cards? Want emails? Want funny pictures on your page? I love you so much, and in some ways you have been a Mom to me as well as my Big Sis, but mostly you've been my confidante, my source of inspiration, my competitor, my equal, and, yeah, my sister. Always my sister. I don't know how or what to feel, other than fear that I'm not doing enough. I don't think I'll ever adjust to you having cancer like this. I'm positive that you are going to do better than anyone else thinks, because we've got that cruise to go on next year! And I won't go if you don't. (No one to compete with on tasting everything, trying everything, seeing everything, etc.) All three of us balance out the extremes of the others of us. I miss our chats. I know we'll have them again soon, because everything is going to get better enough. Right?

I want people to learn that when I say I want to visit and if you come see me I can visit, don't be afraid of my cancer. Why do they have to treat me as if I am too fragile to have friends or people visit? Cancer is not a disease that you can catch from me. I can't find any medical studies that prove you can get cancer by sitting beside a person with cancer.

I'm not sick. I just have cancer. I don't like being treated as if I am someone to be avoided. I feel as if groups of people are using my cancer as an excuse to avoid me. It's as if they are saying, "Let's not go visit Karen, she might not feel good. Too many people around might make her tired." Yes, I will and do get tired. But I still like to be the one to make the decisions for myself.

Why don't individuals allow Jay and me to decide what is best for us? Christie posts a message on my online status, asking, "So other people should just be straight forward and not assume things or try to spare you without at least getting your input first? That's what I got out of your message. So listen up friends of Karen, ask her. If she can she will, if she can't she will let you know! Love you sis!" She put it in perspective!

Chapter 30

Repeat 3-day 2011

I had signed up for the 2011 Susan G. Komen 3-Day Walk. I started to solicit donations online and received my first donation of $25.00 Attending the closing ceremonies of the walk in October reminded me how important it is to be part of funding research to find appropriate medications to treat and cure this disease. With as many people as I am connected with online I know that if each donates less than $5.00 I will exceed the minimum donation required to participate in the actual walk.

I explain that the donations made using the link on my page will go to the Susan G. Komen Foundation on my behalf. I have to raise $2300.00 to have the opportunity to walk 60 miles over a period of three days. As a new Stage 4 Breast Cancer Warrior, I know firsthand how much cancer impacts one's life. It is my goal to not only have earned enough to walk, but to do everything the doctors tell me so that I am alive to attend and participate next year.

The 60 mile walk raised over $75 million dollars in 2009 between all 15 events. Money raised goes towards funding mammograms for those unable to afford them, towards finding a cure, and education. I am only asking for individual donations of $23.00, but any donor can feel free to give more or less based on whatever their hearts tell them to do.

The end result of registering and focusing on getting healthy instead of fundraising. I received a single donation. Just one. No more. Again I'm reminded that as a person with cancer it is about the talk not the walk. One day, I will make a difference in the lives of others, and it may not be through well marketed events.

Chapter 31

I Don't Have an Expiration Date

Weeks have turned into months. I'm still alive and still receiving Hospice care. Each week I have a nurse in to take my vitals and ask how I am feeling. We discuss the medications the other doctors have ordered and the radiation treatments. I mention that the radiation seems to help me feel better and I'm reminded that radiation is not a medical service that will cure me, just one that will reduce my pain and make the process of dying less painful. Again I'm reminded that I should be dying not striving to live. Otherwise today is just another day in the life of cancer. No big deal. So I have cancer, sometimes the cancer hurts, other times I might feel a headache or a stubbed toe. I do pretty good keeping each in their own compartment and do not focus on trying to compare how much "hurt" any individual discomfort is.

I have a MRI scheduled and Jay rearranges his work schedule to take me to the imaging center. For this test I have radioactive isotopes injected into my vein. I am considered to be mildly radioactive and have to avoid seniors, pregnant women and those with lowered immunity. The results will be provided to both of the specialists that are providing my care and to Hospice. There is no expectations of improvements from Hospice.

My Breast Cancer was stage 2 and is now stage 4 and I have bone mets in several locations. The cancer is actually Invasive Ductal Carcinoma, Estrogen Receptor 100% Positive, Progesterone Receptor 97% Positive, HER2 Negative. I feel better, I'm off the oxygen most of the day and no longer using a walker. I have recovered considerably, but, according to Hospice I will be dead before the end of this month.

Thanksgiving is going to be here soon! If I live past Thanksgiving I will have outlived the date that was forecasted for my death. My sister is excited for this holiday also. It will be the first time since her boys were all young and living at home that they will be having the holiday together. Jay, Tina and I are going to spend the day with his parents and it will be a relaxing family day.

Thanksgiving was all I dreamed it would be. Family, football and good food. I'm alive! I beat the odds. I was told I would not be alive at this point in the year. I have beaten the odds. I am a Warrior that uses the Power of Positive Thinking and Prayers to move forward one step at a time! I have a positive attitude! I can live.

Chapter 32

Unexpected Holidays

Trying to decide on what to do for Christmas. I worry about wanting to go to Midnight Mass, while attending will be physically taxing, I know I will spend more mental energy worrying about who is where in relation to my body. Using all that mental energy means that I will get exhausted faster. With all of the people, I will be dodging and sidestepping, Christmas midnight mass will be more taxing than satisfying. The better decision is to not plan on going and to make alternate plans this year.

December is here. I made it through Thanksgiving. I know I will live past Christmas. I feel so much better I have to believe that. No one wants to talk to me about dying except for the Hospice social worker. She has agreed that I might get healthy enough to be discharged from Hospice, but that usually doesn't happen. This month has finals and more medical appointments. I can live through this.

Discussing my death is not something anyone wants to do. Whenever I comment about how hard it is to live I'm told to suck it up buttercup, I've got this and I will beat this. Why is death a taboo discussion? Why do people want to hurry through the days to what will eventually be a certain end that none of us will escape?

It's amazing, there are people who say they will be right there with you the entire way and visit and run the victory speeches. I made it through the semester and still have radiation appointments to go to. I'm still not driving and there is a swelling on my chest. I am so afraid of a septic infection. That's how my mom died: systemic sepsis infection. Reality is people are afraid to be around people who might die. They allow their own busy schedule, to create an excuse to avoid facing mortality. My cancer is not something someone can catch. It's not. My positive attitude is flagging. I hurt. I'm so exhausted and sore. I'm tired of being a burden on my family. I just want to be normal. Will there ever be a normal again? It's becoming ok for people to be unwilling to be around me. I'm learning to accept this as a new normal.

It occurs to me that I need to be careful, not just with what I share but how I share it. Talking about things that are part of my daily life can be off-putting or even frightening to people, even my sister, who lives with us. Metastases are nothing to scoff at, of course, but I have to remember that not everyone understands that infections are potentially deadly and that pain and tumors and radiation are just things I need to deal with now, in order to live longer.

Chapter 33

She Died

Oh Wow. She died. It's real. Breast cancer kills people. No, breast cancer doesn't kill anyone, it is the metastatic disease that really causes the death of the person.

I'm so lucky to be alive.

How long before she becomes just part of history, a forgotten ex-wife of a senator? How long will her name remain as an advocate for breast cancer? When will she be forgotten?

Elizabeth Edwards showed so many women how to live with the disease I now have. I will remember her as a lady of grace and strength and try to carry forward a small part of what she did and who she was. Yes, "was." She is no more on this earth, she is now "past."

When will I be past? What will I leave behind? Will I be forgotten in the future just as I feel forgotten now? Being forgotten is just a temporary part of life. Life itself is very temporary to begin with.

ELIZABETH EDWARDS — You were a lady of grace and strength to the very end. Thank you for being you and being a strong advocate. May you rest in peace beautiful lady.

Elizabeth Edwards, 61, dies after battle with cancer

Elizabeth Edwards, the estranged wife of former North Carolina senator and presidential candidate John Edwards, died Tuesday after a lengthy battle with cancer. She was 61.

Elizabeth Edwards said that cancer will not win the battle because the battle is about "Living a Good Life." Cancer may result in a loss of physical life, but it won't win when we live a good life. Live well, my friends, fellow warriors and survivors!

Chapter 34

Reflections

The 2009 Tampa Three-Day walk. I was tagged today in a post about photos. The photo is ironic. It shows the 3 day banner for photo backgrounds and it says Walking with you got me through Day 3.

Walking with me. That was Thor my standard poodle service dog and another wonderful young lady that was left behind from her team. We were the forgotten three. I could not keep up with the speed of my teammates, I believed I was a hindrance, I allowed my lack of self-confidence to affect the walk. I felt I slowed them down from day one. Before we even reached the first pit stop on the first day I had already told the last one that was walking with me to go ahead and join the rest of the team. I wasn't trying to be a hero. I knew how much those individuals enjoyed being together and I didn't want to feel like my inability was forcing any one of them to have to give up something to be with me.

Strange, I feel that way again here at the end of 2010. Why should I expect or even request that people want to be with me, when I will just slow them down?

When reality finally hits and you realize things you formerly expected to happen might not occur, you make new expectations, change your attitude, and create a bucket list.

My bucket list includes going to Walt Disney World, a ride in a hot air balloon, a flight in a glider, and to spend every precious moment left with those that I am proud to call friends and family. Medical statistics suck and currently have me on a downer, but all of that is part of being a Warrior. During good times and bad times, we fight to live a productive life.

Cancer won't win! The only way it could would be for me to give up living and chose to die. I won't! A friend of mine reminds me that everything depends upon where I place my focus. I shouldn't focus on bad luck, misery, or things I feel are missing from my life. If I do, then those things are the things I will feel the most strongly. I need to change my focus to feeling joy, being grateful for my blessings, and the things I have in abundance.

Chapter 35

All Gain, No Pain

I just cannot believe how GOOD I feel this morning! I can take on the WORLD! Now give me back my darn car keys! And, as long as I do not overdo it, I'll feel this way until tonight! I think I found the med regimen that works and a way to sleep for more than 30 minutes. Life is happy today! I just have two more back treatments to survive and then I have a break for Christmas. It's nice not to cry when I lay down

I still can't overdo it, but I'm on my way to "doing!" YIPPEEE! I just have two more radiation treatments and then I'm done for now. At that point we get to shake it all out and to see what we have. My doctor forecasts many months of low-pain or no-pain days on their way. I think it was her Christmas present to me.

Being in the "mood" for Christmas is so hard. I'm beating the odds for a second time. We were told I would be dead shortly after Thanksgiving. Definitely by Christmas. With Christmas slowly making its way into reality and with my body feeling better, I can almost believe that I will beat the odds all the way. However, other peoples' attitudes seem to make it hard for me to want to participate in the season. I know that reasons exist behind all of these emotions and behaviors. I know, it's hard for everyone involved. I want to rip all the ornaments off my tree and stuff the tree back into its box. I have no tolerance for rudeness right now. Instead, I stuff my anger and disappointment into their "box" and the tree remains where it is.

Chapter 36

Cold or Cancer?

Coughing, Sneezing, hot flashes, and so on. I still have a house I am trying hard to clean with the little energy I have. It's bad enough that there was not much energy to begin with—thank you cancer—but now I have even less. Anyone want to risk a cold and help me clean?

Christie teases me, posting, "Didn't you know that today is National Do Not Clean Your House Day? Shame on you for trying to clean your house on a day like today! You should just sit, relax, sneeze, cough, and Facebook all day! I need a poodle heart!"

She's talking about "Puzzled Hearts" an online game. She tells me how I can send her a poodle heart. I have to remember that for the future, since I had thought I needed to have one in my inventory to send her one.

People send me posts giving me permission not to clean, to sit and relax and enjoy myself. Unfortunately, I have to prepare for a large yard sale. It looks like the bunk bed is sold, the queen bed, and also the sleigh bed set. We still have to sell the white wicker bedroom set and other furniture we no longer need now that we are two people here instead of five. I have to rearrange rooms and empty the dishwasher, get three bathrooms cleaned, and I have tile floors that have not been mopped for months. I don't know when it will get done, but maybe dishwasher will at least get finished today. I post these thoughts, as well.

More teasing: "If Thor is going to be living with you, then he needs to help out around the house. Tell him to get up off his butt and clean the floor and get the bathrooms cleaned so you can relax today."

Thor and Bear keep all dropped food off the floor, and Thor picks up things off the floor for me. That is the most I can get him to do.

I know people mean well. I am being reassured that the house can wait. I need to relax and to kick my cold before I can even think about feeling good enough to clean the entire house. One of my friends posts that she's sorry to hear that I'm sick. She's sitting at doctors with her mom, who is very sick with flu-like symptoms. Not good for someone who has had a kidney transplant. Sympathy? A warning? I had better think about priorities today.

I also know that cleaning the house is at the bottom of my priority list, but I am so tired of dirty floors. It will probably have to wait until Jay can get back to it. Maybe this weekend. Unfortunately, hospice does not provide any assistance with either transportation or housecleaning. They only provide assistance with medical personnel, medications, durable medical equipment, and counseling. For the rest, Jay and I are on our own.

The hospice nurse just left. Both my lungs are raspy but there is no fluid in either of them. I am starting on antibiotics and cough suppressant and increasing breathing treatments. I will be better before the holiday weekend! Yippee! I love Z-packs—they work fast. I feel like whining, but it would not help anyone, even me.

A whole body PET scan is now scheduled for Jan 7. I'm praying that God's will be done and praying his will is no new lights on the film! I get lots of support and encouragement online that the scan will only show improvements.

Christmas is right around the corner. I am getting excited. Expectations may be exceeded!

Chapter 37

Expectations Shattered

Somehow I expected "more" for this Christmas. I don't know more what, but more of something. It feels like just another darn day of the year. I should "feel" something. Maybe gratitude for being alive, or for this wonderful home to live in surround by two fantastic dogs and my wonderful guy?

Sometimes I do things others can't quite understand. I do things that will be better for the person involved and I remove my emotions from the equation. Truly I try hard to put others first and make sure their needs are met before my wants are expressed. It amazes me how situations become about others outside of the event instead of just those involved directly. I promised my mother that I would let Tina make decisions on who she wanted to live with after my mom died. It was hard for me to let go and accept her choice, but it wasn't about me, it was doing what was right for a teenager.

I had expected to have my sister/niece/daughter girl here with us for Christmas. But, she now has chosen to live elsewhere. Her actions and behaviors showed me so very clearly that I was not the person at this time that she needed in her life. I hope she is enjoying today and her Christmas is all that she expected.

Maybe I should feel glad I don't have pain, well not so much that I can't live with it. After all, I'm weaning myself off the morphine since the radiation treatments are working so well. However I feel like the expectations I had for this holiday just are not fitting into what Christmas reality is.

"When Christmas doesn't fit your expectations of what the perfect holiday should be, think about how Joseph and Mary probably didn't think that manger was the perfect place for their child to be born. But look at what a perfect Christmas that turned out to be – Joel Osteen"

Maybe I just need to look deeper. The miracle of Christmas has to be here somewhere inside of me. It's something that I lack, not anyone else's lacking. The miracle of Christmas is in every person you see. I need to take a moment and rejoice in the beauty of that miracle and believe what I am told: You are loved beyond anything you can ever imagine!

Chapter 38

The Start of a New Year

Crown and Coke, grilled steak, steamed veggies and all the fireworks we want out the back windows! May your New Year's Eve be all that you want it to be and may 2011 bring you all the blessings and joys you and your families deserve. Love all my friends and family!

New Year's Eve quietly comes and goes out with lots of fireworks. Jay and I sit outside on our patio and watch all the fireworks that the neighbors and business are shooting off. There are several light displays going off over Tampa Bay and we can see the higher displays. The smell of the gunpowder wafts over to us and brings the experience a full circle.

I made it through the end of the year! I am still alive! I am living! Happy New Year Everyone Near and Far, life is wonderful.

Did you think I wouldn't be alive today? I did. Many times that thought crossed my mind. I'm still here and I have an exciting future ahead of me! Time to start living and taking back my future.

Chapter 39

Things I Wish I Didn't Have To Hear

There are so many statements I wish had never been uttered by others. Some are said out of ignorance or stupidity, and others are spoken because the person believes they will help. It is difficult to know what to say or how to behave when your loved one or friend has cancer. I can't speak for everyone as our sensitivities are different, but for me the following words and actions only drive a wedge into my interactions with others.

My top of the list "never say" statement was said out of love and with true belief that it would make me feel much more comfortable. "It's ok to die; I'll take care of your family for you." It's never truly ok to die, but acknowledging that you will die and discussing that helps make that transition easier. Many people believe, as do I, that permission to die is necessary as is forgiveness. The fault in the statement wasn't that it was ok to die, but that another person would step in and replace me in my family's lives. That statement alone became more motivation to live. When the time comes, please tell me that it is ok to die, but finish that with you will be ok! Please only accept the responsibility for yourself and those children that live at home with you.

Don't assume that I am unable to participate in an activity. Ask me; just be willing to hear me say, "No, I can't do that." I might surprise you and truly be able to take that hike with you or proofread a manuscript for you. Don't limit me because you are trying to help me live longer. Treat me the same way you did before I had cancer or as if I did not have cancer. Don't allow the cancer to control our relationship.

Speaking of the word no; it is ok for me to not share information, or answer questions, or even have visitors. I do as much as I am comfortable with doing, as many others with cancer do. Many days or weeks we push ourselves while we feel good so that we can experience more life.

A tough one for most people is to not tell me that you understand how I feel. At the same time I also many times do not want to hear that you could never understand how I feel. While you may not be able to understand my physical condition, you can empathize when I explain how it feels. You can understand how I am mentally adjusting to every change when you listen to what I describe. Deciding that you cannot understand indicates a lack of willingness to want to be involved.

One of the best lessons I learned was when a friend said to me, I can do this or this to help as it is what I am good at. Would that help you? She was very specific and then she followed through and did that which she offered to do. It was a simple gift; she gave our two dogs a bath, and drove me to an appointment. It was truly greatly appreciated and one of the most memorable interactions I had with my friends after diagnosis.

Everyone has a different experience with cancer. My cancer is not the same as the lady next to me in the chemo lounge getting treatment for her breast cancer. Our medications make our experience different as does how our bodies react to it. We can understand the experience of being told that cancer now exists in our bodies. We can understand that someone has negative side effects. It is our responsibility to share that understanding without imposing our will on another. Please don't tell me that when my treatment is over, I will feel better. Without knowing, you just made me feel as if you were approving my death.

Please do not tell me that if I would exercise more, or eat this plant or that plant, or move to this state or that country I could be healed. I am working with experts in the field that have an intimate knowledge of my health and the progress of my cancer. The claims on the internet do not take into the equation the state of my current condition. Chasing miracle cures takes away time from those I love and want to be with. I also don't want to disappoint you for not taking your suggestion seriously enough.

Many of those I have as online friends also have chronic or invisible medical conditions. I asked them to share what they dislike hearing as well as what they would like to hear. I believe it is important to share their thoughts also.

The predominant answer has been, "you don't look sick, what's wrong with you?" Frankly, we all do our best to not "look" like anything and as if there is nothing is wrong with us. We are not obligated to tell anyone our medical condition. Just accept that today is not a good day and we used almost all our energy just to "look good" because sometimes looking good helps us just feel better. Just because we "look great" doesn't mean you have to follow up with "I would have never thought you were going through that."

We don't want to know about your disease, not as a competition. None of us are here to be in competition with another. I accept that you have a medical condition, but your condition does not diminish how mine makes me feel. Please respect me and don't try to compare.

The most outrageous statement I was asked to share was when an individual made a comment in a discussion that she had to go for treatment, the "friend" she was talking with said she understood that she had to go get her Mercedes detailed. Comparing health care to car care? I believe that statement takes the credit for most outrageous one I have ever heard.

I tend to upset people. I'm not sick. I just have cancer. When I'm sick I'll let you know. There are so many other things that can be said if people knew, cared or even thought about it.

Don't tell me I can't do and to sit down and let you do. All that does is make you feel better about helping when you are really just causing me to feel disabled. Your decisions to take over activities I can do limit my ability to feel productive and normal. Your behavior will condition me to not try to do anything when you are around. After all you have limited or no confidence in my skills and abilities to do that activity. Why should I try when you think so little of my ability? I'll just find something else to do. Eventually, I will resent you as a result of your limiting me.

I asked again on Facebook for what those with invisible disabilities would like to hear from family and friends. The same group of men and women that responded to what they don't want to hear responded to what they do want to hear. Their comments mirror my thoughts so I'll share more of theirs than mine.

My friends want to be told that they are living with grace and dignity. They are not doing more than anyone else, they just want to be recognized that they are doing the best they are able in their unique circumstance and that they are normal. Please take the time to express that you understand how they feel. You may not "know" the same pain, but you do understand the concept of pain.

While cancer has its signals that you are getting treatment it is still mostly an invisible disease. For those that have an *invisible* disease it's nice when people don't treat us like it's all in our head, or if we just took the right supplement or followed this miracle diet, we'd be fine, trust us, many tried everything, some for over twenty years, with some but never complete success. What would be truly nice is for the medical community to take invisible disabilities seriously. It is a debilitating, even crippling disease whose effects ripple out as with all chronic illnesses to affect family and friends.

I want people to recognize that I'm not 100 percent capable and just slow down and smell the pretty flowers sometimes. There are good days and bad days, but on both I think I don't want to hear anything about how I'm doing. At the same time I know it helps to talk about it. I guess I wouldn't mind answering questions. So maybe what I want to hear is someone trying to understand or wanting to educate themselves about me. Or maybe just asking me how I feel or I'm doing or dealing with it. Sometimes it's obvious I guess.

I would love it if they called sometime and just chat about what is going on in my life or theirs! To not be forgotten or invisible! To ask to meet for lunch or play cards or whatever! Something other than focus on health! Please ask how can I help? (And mean it be willing to follow through).

Chapter 40

Facing Death Decisions

When I finally die, and I will, the question remains of how to help those I leave behind honor my legacy and be strong. My family has the strength to overcome much. I have seen it so many times in the past, in my war on cancer and how they have handled the traumas in their lives. From a grandchild that endured a traumatic lawn mower accident to another misdiagnosed by several doctors for Kawasaki Disease to two daughters that had to go through domestic issues that resulted in upheaval and relocation of their homes to do what was in the best interests of their children, just as I did. My children have the strength of warriors and they will not just survive my death, but incorporate it into their lives and move forward with courage and conviction becoming better ladies.

My children and Jay's children already know that when they are needed he will let them know. He will have the support of our families and they will help him make it through the days until he is ready to continue his life journey by himself, or with others.

My friends can help them by listening and sharing memories or stories of times they spent with me. They can bring food immediately after and help with any planning that may be needed. Offer what your skills are and then follow through. Communicate and share. That is how you can help.

There are many websites that give advice on how to help a friend that is grieving. I don't need to repeat any of it. But I would ask that everyone remember that individual grief is not on a "timeframe." Some openly grieve for hours, days or weeks and others silently grieve for years. Allow my loved ones and those that loved me the time to grieve. Don't tell them it has been long enough and they need to move on. Let them decide when they are ready to move to the next step. They deserve that respect and so do I.

That being said, no I'm not planning on stopping my treatment and trotting off into the sunset to die. I've just started living. I have much left to enjoy, work to do, and children to watch grow up.

Life is meant to be enjoyed. We are not here to trudge through each day without a smile and love. We are all worthy of being loved. We all deserve to find something that brings a smile to our faces.

I was asked why I survived a death sentence. I believe that life with cancer is not about only doctors and medications; it is about having a bit of luck, a bit of faith, a bit of courage, and the attitude that living is what I was going to do. Attitude and determination made the difference. Living is a decision. How a person lives is also a decision. You can make the decision to let life happen and be miserable or you can chose to decide to live and enjoy it.

A positive attitude about the small things in life will make a big difference in each day. How are you going to live your life? How will you handle a chronic medical condition? Where will you go from this point in your life? Take some risks, live life as fully as you can. Don't wait for someday to do this or that.

Tim McGraw sang the song "Live Like You Are Dying". I recognize many similarities between my life and his song. I was in my early 40's when I was first diagnosed with cancer. I had a lot of life before me. For a moment, I was stopped on a dime. I spent several days looking at medical reports and talking about options and believing that this could be the end of what I knew life to be. I had to choose what to do. I chose to live. Four years later I heard the words that I was dying, there was no turning back the clock. Reality sunk in: it really hits you when you get that kind of news. You have to decide what you are going to do. I did. I went to school, I went to Washington D.C., I spent time with our grandchildren and our children, I enjoyed my friends, I loved more, and I forgave those I had been unwilling to forgive before. I recognized that not everyone will get to live like they are dying. They won't understand the true concept of today very well will be the last day they will ever live. They won't know the thoughts one who does know, thinks as they lay their head down and cover up for the night. They don't truly understand the meaning of I woke up today, I am blessed and so very lucky.

I have learned to love deeper, speak sweeter, and forgive freely. I hope you get the chance without having to get a diagnosis of impending death. Become the person you would like to be, the spouse your love wants you to be, it isn't such an imposition. Take the time to read a good book or go fishing. Take a good long hard look that song Tim McGraw sings of and look to see if what you are doing is what you would do again, if you knew you were dying. Go ahead. Live like you are dying. You can do it.

Chapter 41

Looking Back

It's been four months that I have lived with metastatic cancer. I have exceeded medical expectations. I did not settle in and die, I fought to do one step more every day to keep living.

I have invasive breast cancer, which is only seen in about twelve percent of all individuals who develop breast cancer. Of those individuals who are treated early, only thirty percent develop into a metastatic condition, or Stage IV. Only twenty-two percent of that thirty percent will live past the five-year post diagnosis date. Using the SEER database it is projected that breast cancer will result in 232,670 new cases this year. Of those cases, 27,920 will be invasive breast cancer. From them, 8,376 will develop metastatic disease. Only 1,842 of all those women will live to see their fifth anniversary with metastatic disease, this is less than .8% of all diagnosed breast cancer cases. These numbers are pretty stark.

Another statistical factor is that one third of all individuals discharged from hospice die within six months. I haven't lived the last four months, thinking about survival statistics. Neither am I going to live my future thinking about them. It is important for others to recognize that individuals with metastatic breast cancer are living life with a limited number of days. The vast majority of those individuals do not live as if they are dying. Rather, they live.

I found a list of New Year's Resolutions. It is my last list. This list is one that will always need to be repeated as there will always be room for improvement. If I could remember who created these ideas I would send them a large thank you. I made some small modifications to make it fit me.

My Sixteen New Year's Resolutions for 2011 and Beyond!

I will appreciate my family, and friends, for whom they are, what they mean to me and others, and to gracefully overlook some things they do (or don't do). None of us is perfect and accepting that reality is a good thing for relationships to flourish.

I will act upon wrongs that need righting, crass statements that require correction and offenses that demand just responses. I will set a positive example by not accepting negativity in others. I will endeavor to right those wrongs no matter where I find them.

I will be a valuable teammate and to trust others to do their best. I should know what position I play, and regularly practice my skills to do my personal best. I do not always have to lead.

I will actively listen to the voices of children and elders. The wisdom of innocence and experience is both free and priceless.

I will attempt to always speak the truth to power, but to be both polite and persistent. There's a fine line between persistence and pestilence. Resist aggressiveness, but advocate with assertion, confidence and commitment to the cause, no matter what cause I take up.

I will accept that I don't know everything. By finding others who know much more, together we can create a great brain trust and blend expertise. Knowledge of a group is stronger than that of an individual.

I will try to pleasantly surprise someone every day with a genuine smile and unexpected kindness in word and deed. Life's subtle gifts of concern are cherished.

I will respect and celebrate the diversity of faiths, feelings, and fashions. Differences are natural and honoring each other's beliefs creates mutual admiration.

I will exercise and appreciate artistic expression for its intrinsic value. The vitality of the instrumental, literary, dance, visual or vocal arts fuels the soul and expands the mind to new possibilities. I will expand my exposure to artistic expression.

127

I will invest a thoughtful minute before I speak or act. Regret is often preventable. Reversing harm is one of life's most vexing challenges.

I will honor those who courageously sacrifice for us at home and abroad, care for our health, educate, protect us and perform the healing and helping arts so that our quality of life is improved.

I will share even if I think I don't have enough. Setting an example by gifting to others in need is one of the best lessons for children to observe. Even when all I can share is my time.

I will protect, defend and advocate for people who rely on me. Give special attention to the needs of others who may not know how to find their own voice.

I will preserve natural environments for their beauty and bounty. Natural settings are home to plant life and species which are too often victims of our wants not needs. I will stop and smell the flowers and enjoy the stars.

I will never give up on a person or a cause, despite the challenges I face. Perseverance is an attitude that exemplifies leadership, attracts allies, and creates meaningful change. Like my health challenges I will persevere for my family and friends in their causes when I can.

I will never give up on myself. I will take responsibility for my actions, my body and my health. I will improve the condition of my body through better health, eating and exercise.

I will appreciate my family, friends, and colleagues for whom they are, what they mean to me and others, and to gracefully overlook some things they do (or don't do). None of us is perfect and accepting that reality is a good thing for relationships to flourish. I will not blame my friends when we grow apart and our paths diverge. They have the right to grow and move forward on different journeys.

I am able to take these goals and implement them into my life. They can become second nature and continue to be refined and improved as the years go by. That was my resolution.

Looking back at the challenges I had to face is tough. The

challenges and changes my loved ones had to overcome exceeded the ones I faced. My love, the man who brought me back from falling into the center of the earth during the psychotic event from medication at the hospital, had to transform from lover to caregiver. I left the hospital totally dependent on others for my all of my basic care. I could not dress myself, shower, and get out of bed or onto and off of the commode without assistance. I was completely dependent. I truly could do nothing for myself much less for my family.

Jay was the one who took care of all my needs. Hospice did not offer that level of care. Jay's day began at four o'clock in the morning, when he would get up and prepare for the day. By six o'clock in the morning, he was helping me begin mine. My mornings began with bathroom trips, medications, shower, dressing, and breakfast. Then Jay would help me to the recliner where I would spend the morning while he was working, cleaning, and caring for the home. A few weeks later I was able to use the walker and get to the bathroom by myself and Jay was able to return to work. After all of this, he would continue the morning activities and leave for work, but by lunch time he would be home again to make my lunch help me with mid-day activities and then drive the thirty minutes back to work for the afternoon. His cell phone was always within reach and there would be hourly telephone calls to make sure that I was still ok. Before the work day was complete Jay was driving home early to start dinner and help me prepare for the evening. His evening activities included grocery shopping, laundry, caring for our pets, meal preparation, and my personal care while he still had to find time to rest so he could be at work.

Cancer and caregiving are as much of a challenge and as exhausting as cancer and surviving are. Without Jay, I would not be here today. He is and was my strength and my white knight. In spite of being told I was going to die, he continued to treat me as if I was going to live. Death was not an option that we were going to consider. Living was the only option. Jay worked hard to ensure that I would live. I will always remember being too weak to eat and he put food on the fork and fed me so that I could get the nutrients I needed to live. I was like an infant for a period of time. As my abilities increased and my

129

strength returned I was able to take on more of the personal care responsibilities for myself. Even at this point in my life there are still simple home chores that I am physically unable to do or cause me pain when I do them. Jay continues to do those home chores without complaint. He shares with me how glad he is I am alive and spending my life with him. I may be dependent on help for living, but I am not treated as a burden. I never was.

The question I have found most interesting was how I want friends to celebrate my life after I die. I've decided that I don't want them to celebrate my life after I die. Why bother? I want them to celebrate my life while I'm alive. Take the time now to tell me what you appreciate about me. Don't wait until I'm dead. I can't hear you then. Join me for a big shindig of a party. Let's have music, food, dancing and a great time. We can do it before I choose to stop my treatment so that I may fully enjoy my time with you. I do not understand why anyone would want to wait to say those things about their loved instead of saying it to their loved one.

I do not look forward to telling our children that we have decided to stop my treatments and allow the natural process of death to take over. One day that will be required. I have already discussed with them that I will make that decision in the future. They have all agreed to support my decision and be available for us at that time. I have been told that at that point, it will be all about what my needs are. Until then we are all going to live our lives independently and care for those we live with and love. Parents must concentrate on their children, our grandchildren now.

When it's time to end my treatments I've already made the plans for how I want to die. Jay and I are going to go to the beach and enjoy every sunset until I can't enjoy them any longer. In his arms and with his love surrounding me I will allow myself to transition from this world to that which is beyond my understanding. We are going to enjoy wine, walking in the surf and holding hands. The time together will be exclusively ours. When it appears to be my final few days, our children will be invited to come and say goodbye. But it should not be a tearful time. Instead I would like it to be a time where we reflect on the joys we have had together.

My future holds a great adventure! I'm not sure where it is going or how it will unfold, but I know that it will be exciting. I had started a bucket list and then I decided that was a waste of time. I'm going to embrace every opportunity for adventure and every challenge that heads my way. Life isn't about just the things that should be done before you die, it is about the lives you impact and the things you do every day. A smile or kind word can go a long way to improving the day of another, and it also improves yours at the same time.

I am excited about living. I intend to thrive and experience all that I am able.

I am planning on becoming the best person I can be within the boundaries of the new normal I live; no matter how many times those normal changes. I will expand my energy to being able to contribute more towards the running of our home life. I will learn what type of exercises I can do that will not cause exhaustion. I will enjoy the time spent with children and grandchildren. I will be here for my friends. I am choosing to be a mentor for those that are newly diagnosed with metastatic disease. I will learn how to help others live fully.

This is just the beginning of the rest of my life!

Don't Miss

Jungle Mystic

JULY 2015

Jungle Mystic

Chapter One

Autumn hung on the spiraling wind currents. The ground littered with the discarded garments of the mighty oaks, now threadbare and skeletal. The senescing was complete and all that remained was for the mighty winter to decompose their discarded garments. Every footstep, placed to limit the sound that would alert others. Increasing his speed to a trot, the sounds of a waterfall drew closer. The water cascaded over the lip of the cliff and shattered on the rocks below before it flowed into a pool surrounded by boulders. Ascending to the lip of the cliff, extended in each reach, his muscles rippled. Surveying the domain for a moment he roared sounding like a beast of the ancient past. Flexing his body, he dove off the cliff into the pool below, swimming to the boulders, he rested his head as he waited for her to arrive. His golden eyes were alert to all movement in the Jungle and for a few moments he is drawn to the memories of the past.

Many millenniums ago a group of elders and high priests traveled through the portals to planet Earth as it entered its Ice Age. Each continent sent one elder and one priest to retrieve an animal to Anju to continue the life. They could not allow all the animals and plants on planet Earth to perish in the bitter cold. From the steppes of Siberia the Giant Wooly Mammoth was chosen, the jungles gave forth the

Machairodus. The first trip to Planet Earth to retrieve these animals created more questions than the beasts they brought back. Decisions had to be made on what type of creatures to save and how many. The portal would be able to take the essence of the animal and create a mate for it, so was it necessary to have more than one of any given beast? Would the portal create mates for such powerful beasts and how would they control them?

From the Gobi Desert in Mongolia on Planet Earth the elder and priests gathered a Gallimimus. This beaked Ornithomimed was a 17 foot long omnivore, he would not cause any damage to the humans on the planet and would in turn be cared for and given safe passage when he wanted to travel outside the planet's atmosphere.

Hungary and Romania was where the Titanosaurud Sauropod was found. This 27 foot gentle creature was an herbivore and chose the tastiest and most flavorful greens available.

From the oceans the 13 feet Archelon was gathered to transport to Anju. Its paddle like limbs made it difficult to catch under the water. The horny plates protected it from the many meat eating predators.

These giants among animals were the first attempt to collect animals and bring them through the portal, they were however, unable to split their essence as the planet did not have a single Magi to aid in the transformation and reassignment program in Anju. The quest for a Magi for each country on the planet would have to continue.

Over many centuries, Magi children were discovered and brought in the instant of death through the portal to the country that most resembled the lands they lived in on the planet earth. They were brought up in a family home and raised to be children of Anju. With the exception of the magi skills the first children grew up simply. As the generations increased so did the knowledge of what the magi child would be able to do for her lands. The child was always a female and there was not any rhyme or reason to the order of birth of the child.

Many threats had impacted Anju over the millenniums the planet has seen land masses join and then separate, intense periods of heat and cold, loss of animal and plant life and even threats from people on other planets in their solar system. Saberzahn remembered the men arriving and bringing him to this land. He was the last of the giants to have a magic child assigned to his care.

The call from the wizard was strong, he would not ignore it. Leaping from the pond and took off at a full run. Leaping over logs, and crashing through the brush. He cared not that he was creating havoc in his wake, he only focused on getting to the wizard as fast his long strides would take him. Sliding on the ground, he slid to the wizard's feet. Standing, he shook the dirt and branches off and looked questioning into the cave. A thin-film glimmered and showed the passage way to the planet that he once lived on. It was a place called Earth, in the solar system the Milky Way. Life is much easier now than it was then.

Through the cave of portals a village and the events begin to unfold causing his anger and frustration. Would the earth people ever learn? Their actions are destroying lives of other humans and the land around them. The heat is so intense the flames are blue and white. An entire village, consumed by the flames as the Knights of Templars gathers what valuables they can from the village. Destruction is complete in this village, none survive. The flames advance and consume all vegetation. Trees topple as bushes crackle the fire is beyond the control of those who started it. They follow in the wake to collect precious gems and metals that survive beyond the flames.

He watches the child, a girl, flee the flames. Panic, etched on her face, as she stumbles up the rocky cliff to the cave. She follows the animals and an innate sense of direction, guided by the creatures that race past her.

The child is at the edge of the cave, tears rolling down her cheeks as the fire continues to consume the land she knows as her only home. Her chest heaves as she sobs, her family was unable to leave and they perished in the flames. Her village, and those that lived in the village, as many others before, destroyed. The flames finally drive the girl child in the cave where she finds refuge with the wild animals that have retreated there. Injuries abound with the animals and with a gentle touch she checks each animal and soothes them. Distracted

135

from her loss by focusing on the animals, her grief, forgotten for now.

Two pairs of keen eyes watched the girl child heal the animals. The magic flowed from her fingertips as wounds closed and burns eliminated. The pure magical power was rare for one so young. She would face death by the Knights that were following after the flames. This child needed protection. The wizard turned to his companion and with an unspoken word communicated the need to save the child. Anger overwhelmed him and he started to charge through the portal to save the child. A warm hand on his shoulder halted his forward motion.

The wizard spoke: "We must retrieve her, stay here and I will travel to bring her back. She will be your responsibility to protect for the rest of her life. Beyond her will be many of her descendants and as long as they live, so will you. Her magic will continue through the generations. They will give you strength and power to continue to protect them. Wait here, I will return with your child."

Warmth infused his body and peace replaced the agitation. He was her protector, the protector of the magical child and her children. No longer would he wander in this world he, like others of his kind, now he was charged with a powerful responsibility.

The wizard changed his garments to that of an elder Druid. It would give the girl confidence in traveling to his world. The Druids believed in the Otherworld. They thought the realms were only achieved upon their death, or when in a deep spiritual state. It might prove a challenge for the child to adapt to her new world.

Rohesia watched in terror as the mounted warriors advanced on her hiding spot. She wasn't afraid to die, but she was not ready to travel to the Otherworld. Her plants and animals needed her to survive, she was a healer. Steel on steel clanking as the men rode closer, the cave was her last opportunity to hide. Sobbing, she ran into the cave and fell to the floor. She begged the spirits of the Otherworld to allow her to stay hidden from view. Warm breath blew on her neck as the lion exhaled, injured in the flames and needed the touch of her hand for restoring health. Distracted from her fear she began to heal the animals that had also sought refuge in the cave.

A shimmering mass of light appeared in the back. An elder Druid advanced out of the light. Immediately Rohesia felt that her request granted, she would not die by the hands of the knights on this day. The elder has a deep, warm melodic voice, "Come, my child, we must get you away before the men get here. Gather your friends and let us leave this place of death."

Looking around at the animals and she began to gather them together to leave. She needed to look out the mouth of the cave to gather any stragglers. Fear flew into her breast; the men were so close, only paces away. She knew she must hurry. Turning to the elder, she flew into his arms with tears pouring down her cheeks. "Please, help me gather the animals. We must leave for I can see the crosses on their chest." Following the elder all the animals and Rohesia fled through the light to the Otherworld.

Sabelzahn watched the child and animals step out of the time portal. Now she was his to protect. He stood up to his full height; any humans from Earth that followed would die before they could harm her. His long legs allowed him to move close to her. He put his face near hers, startling her, and spoke to her. "I am your protector, I will guard you with my life, you, my dear child will never know fear again."

Rohesia found comfort in his size and strength.

ABOUT THE AUTHOR

Karen Lewandowski is a highly visible symbol of personal victory over cancer, a source of encouragement and support for her community and an ambassador sharing the inspiration of living with cancer. Karen is engaged to the joy of her life, Jay, and has 5 daughters and has 12 grandchildren. When she isn't encouraging others she can be found experiencing life full strength forward.

WANT MORE?

VISIT

ONESPECIALLADY.COM

FOR NEWS, EXCERPTS AND NEW RELEASES

Made in the USA
Lexington, KY
29 August 2015